IT HAPPENED IN WASHINGTON

To Bill Gulick
The Dean of Washington Writers

CONTENTS

CONTENTS

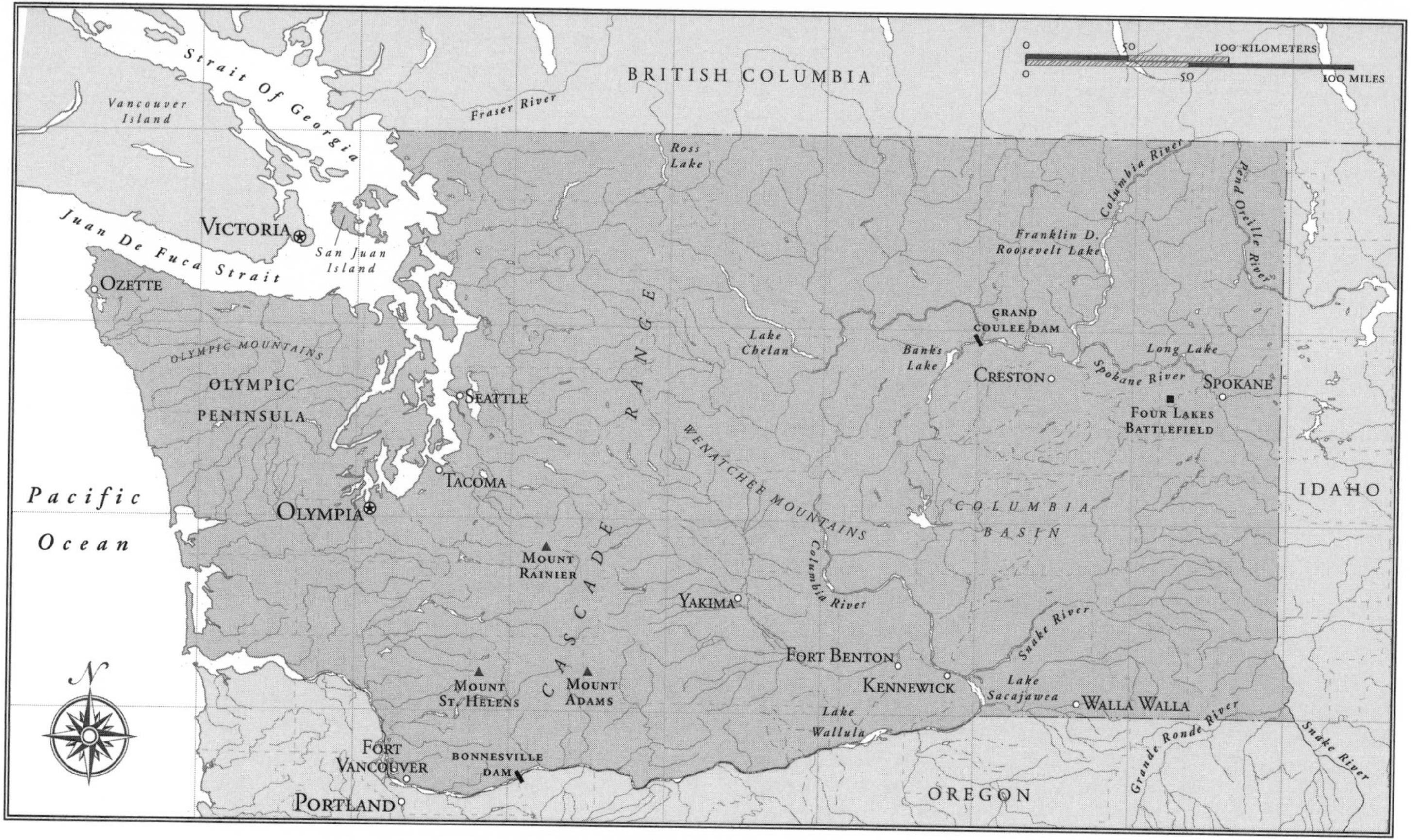

BRITISH COLUMBIA
0 50 100 KILOMETERS
0 50 100 MILES
Strait Of Georgia
Vancouver Island
Fraser River
Ross Lake
VICTORIA
San Juan Island
Juan De Fuca Strait
OZETTE
OLYMPIC MOUNTAINS
OLYMPIC PENINSULA
SEATTLE
TACOMA
OLYMPIA
Pacific Ocean
CASCADE RANGE
WENATCHEE MOUNTAINS
Lake Chelan
MOUNT RAINIER
MOUNT ST. HELENS
MOUNT ADAMS
FORT VANCOUVER
PORTLAND
BONNESVILLE DAM
YAKIMA
Columbia River
FORT BENTON
KENNEWICK
Lake Wallula
Lake Sacajawea
WALLA WALLA
Snake River
Grande Ronde River
OREGON
IDAHO
COLUMBIA BASIN
Banks Lake
GRAND COULEE DAM
CRESTON
Franklin D. Roosevelt Lake
Columbia River
Pend Oreille River
Long Lake
Spokane River
SPOKANE
FOUR LAKES BATTLEFIELD

WASHINGTON

PREFACE

This book highlights several interesting episodes of Washington history, from prehistoric days through modern times. Each story is complete in itself and can be read individually and out of sequence.

Washington is an important state historically, and although the vignettes related in this book do not in any way purport to be a thorough history of the state, they have been selected to give the reader a broad understanding of the varied historical background of the Evergreen State.

I hope that *It Happened in Washington* will provide a few hours of pleasure to those who read it, and that it will find its way into the classrooms of the state, thereby giving younger generations a better appreciation of their vast heritage.

AVALANCHE AT OZETTE

- CIRCA 1480 -

Torrential rain had visited the area daily that spring. In fact, the several hundred natives who lived on what is today Cape Flattery had seen heavy rains for decades. Despite the extreme weather, the people of the small village bustled about doing their daily chores.

Now known as the Makah, these people belonged to the American Indian culture called Northwest Coast and were kin to the Nootka tribesmen of Vancouver Island. They were specifically known as the "People who live on the cape by the rocks and seagulls." Their village was nestled between the Strait of Juan de Fuca and the Pacific Ocean.

That day several men were busy carving a new canoe. The craft, hewed from a giant cedar trunk, measured a full thirty feet long and was capable of carrying eight men with their whaling gear. While children played with a small white dog, women cooked the evening meal of seal meat, salmon, and rock oysters.

Situated a few hundred feet from the Pacific shore were several longhouses, the Makah people's residences. Some of these multifamily houses measured almost seventy feet long and forty-six feet wide.

The exteriors were covered with wide clapboards made from the huge cedar trees native to the area.

The Makah people made their living from the rich waters of the Pacific Ocean. Proficient in hunting even the giant whale from their huge hand-carved canoes, the people of the Northwest Coast also were blessed with large populations of seal, salmon, crab, oyster, and many other kinds of fish, crustaceans, and mammals.

That day, as the pungent smell of smoking salmon and the sweet fragrance from the cooking fires escaped into the cool spring air, a woman screamed. Pointing frantically at the cliffs behind the village, she ran through the ranks of the working people, shouting that a huge mud slide was approaching them. Before anyone had a chance to escape, tons and tons of oozing mud covered the entire village. Like a latter-day Pompeii, most of the Makah village was submerged in a thick layer of mud. Within minutes, what had been a healthy, vibrant village of happy workers was now a jumble of mud, trees, house planks, and debris. Life had been snuffed out of many of the inhabitants.

Parts of the Makah village were preserved exactly as they were when the devastating mud slide occurred. The discovery of artifacts by hikers in 1970 and careful excavation of the site by Washington State University archaeologists have allowed much to be reconstructed about the lifestyles of these advanced Indians who fished the bountiful Pacific waters. Over an eleven-year period, from 1970 until 1981, entire houses, complete with their furnishings, were excavated. Thousands of artifacts, including ropes, tools, canoes, harpoons, cooking gear, baskets, weapons—in all more than fifty thousand objects—were unearthed, making the Ozette site, as it is called today, one of the most incredible and important archaeological finds in North America.

In addition to the evidence found at Ozette during the 1970s, historical documentation sheds light on the lifestyle of these early

Indians who inhabited the coastlines of Washington, Oregon, British Columbia, and Alaska. In 1778 John Ledyard sailed to the Pacific Northwest with Captain James Cook. Several years later, at the suggestion of Thomas Jefferson, Ledyard attempted to cross the North American continent from west to east, starting at Nootka Sound. He has left us a vivid description of the Northwest Coast culture. In the journal of his service with Cook, Ledyard wrote a description of the Makahs' close relatives, the Nootka, who today prefer the name Nu-chah-nulth.

> *I had no sooner beheld these Americans than I set them down for the same kind of people that inhabited the opposite side of the continent. They are rather above the middle stature, copper-coloured, and of an athletic make. They have long black hair, which they generally wear in a club on the top of the head, they fill it when dressed with oil, paint and the downe of birds. They also paint their faces red, blue and white colours . . . Their clothing generally consists of skins, but they have two other sorts of garments, the one is made of the inner rind of some sort of bark twisted and united together like the woof of our coarse cloaths, the other . . . is . . . principally made with the hair of their dogs, which are mostly white, and of the domestic kind: Upon this garment is displayed very naturally the manner of their catching the whale—we saw nothing so well done by a savage in our travels . . . We saw them make use of no coverings to their feet or legs, and it was*

> *seldom they covered their heads: When they did it was with a kind of basket covering made after the manner of the Chinese . . . hats.*

Today many of the thousands of artifacts unearthed at the Ozette site reside in a new home, the Makah Cultural and Research Center Museum on Neah Bay. Nearby, several hundred Makah Indians still call the region home, many of them employed by the new multimillion-dollar Makah Fisheries Company.

CAPTAIN JAMES COOK ON THE WASHINGTON COAST

- 1778 -

It was Sunday, March 22, 1778, and the seas were running high. The weather was cold and bleak, the skies dark and foreboding. As the eminent British sailor Captain James Cook observed the Washington coastline from his ship, HMS *Resolution,* he no doubt felt weary from the many years of exploration he had performed for his government. Although he was only fifty years old, this latest expedition to find the fabled "Northwest Passage" was Cook's third extensive yoyage in ten years. On his previous journeys Cook had logged well over one hundred thousand miles and at the same time gained the respect and admiration of his government.

At this very moment, on the other side of the continent, the ancestors of the people who would one day make their homes in this vast western wilderness that Cook was viewing were fighting his own countrymen in the American Revolution. Since Cook had left England on July 12, 1776, just eight days after the signing of the Declaration of Independence by the American colonies, he probably knew very little at all about the progress of the war.

Cook had sighted the North American landmass some two weeks earlier when he reached the Oregon coastline from the Sandwich Islands, today's Hawaiian chain. Searching for a harbor, he pointed the *Resolution* south toward California. Failing to find a suitable place to land, he turned his ship back north and skirted the Oregon and Washington coastlines. Cook wrote in his journal that the land was

> *of a moderate height, though, in some places, it rises higher within. It was diversified with a great many rising grounds and small hills; many of which were entirely covered with tall, straight trees, and others, which were lower, and grew in spots like coppices; but the interspaces, and sides of many of the rising grounds, were clear.*

Cook's journey up the coast was accompanied by snow and sleet. The captain was troubled that none of the straits that other explorers had reported to be present in these latitudes were visible. On March 22 he wrote in his journal, "it is in this very latitude where we now were that geographers have placed the pretended strait of Juan de Fuca." Yet he was indeed in the neighborhood of the fabled strait, since he had just sighted and named Cape Flattery, which along with Vancouver Island guards the strait on its western end.

Cook and his crew were not aware that the Strait of Juan de Fuca was not discovered by de Fuca at all. However, de Fuca, a Greek explorer sailing for the Spanish, had boasted that he found the famous Northwest Passage in 1592, and since that day most seafarers had assumed that the Greek had really sailed as far north as the strait.

An Englishman, John Meares, actually discovered the entrance to Puget Sound in 1788, but out of respect for de Fuca, who he thought had been there two hundred years earlier, he named the waterway after the Greek captain.

Other navigators had sailed along Washington's coast before Cook. Just three years before, Bruno Heceta, a Spaniard, had skirted the Olympic Peninsula, and later, dropping south due to an Indian fight, he almost discovered the Columbia River. In his journal he noted a change in the color of the sea, and he suggested that it was due to a large body of water discharging into the Pacific. He continued:

> *Having arrived opposite this bay at six in the evening, and placed the ship nearly midway between the two capes, I sounded and found bottom in four brazas [twenty-two feet]. The currents and eddies were so strong that, notwithstanding the press of sail, it was difficult to get out clear of the northern cape [Cape Disappointment], towards which the current ran, though its direction was eastward in consequence of the tide being at flood. These currents and eddies caused me to believe that the place is the mouth of some great river, or of some passage to another sea. Had I not been certain of the latitude of this bay . . . I might easily have believed it to be the passage discovered by Juan de Fuca in 1592. . . . I did not enter and anchor in this port . . . notwithstanding my strong desire to do so.*

Captain Cook did not linger along the Washington coast. Instead he continued northward up the coast of British Columbia to

Alaska. Along the way he ran into several delegations of Northwest Coast Indians, who paddled out to meet him in huge dugout canoes, many of them elaborately carved. At the bow of one was "a singular head, which had a bird's eye and bill, of an enormous size." Cook's crew traded with the Indians for sea otter skins that were "certainly softer and finer than that of any others we know of."

After sailing through the Bering Strait and exploring the Arctic Ocean, Cook turned southward and headed once again for the Sandwich Islands. It was there that the great navigator met his end. Cook's remains were buried at sea on February 21, 1779.

THE CLAIMING OF THE COLUMBIA

- 1792 -

On April 17, 1792, George Vancouver made a mistake that helped shape the destiny of the Pacific Northwest. The British sea captain's government had ordered him to meet with Spanish authorities about spheres of influence around the Nootka Islands. At the same time he was to determine whether any great river of the region emptied into the Pacific Ocean.

In 1778 Vancouver's countryman Captain James Cook had sailed right by the mouth of the Columbia River in his search for a Northwest Passage—a waterway connecting the Pacific and Atlantic Oceans. A Spaniard, Bruno Heceta, thought he might have discovered the "great river" in 1775, but his crew was too sick with scurvy to investigate whether it was a river or a bay.

As Vancouver steered his ship, HMS *Discovery,* past Cape Disappointment, he noted in his log that

> *on the south side of the promontory was the appearance of an inlet or small river, the land behind not indicating*

> *it to be of any great extent; nor did it seem accessible for vessels of our burthen, as the breakers extended from the above point, two or three miles into the ocean, until they joined those on the beach nearly four leagues further south.*
>
> *The Sea had now changed from its natural, to river-coloured water; the probable consequences of some streams falling into the bay, or into the ocean to the north of it, through the low land. Not considering this opening worthy of more attention, I continued our pursuit to the N.W., being desirous of embracing the prevailing breeze.*

And so, in a masterstroke of miscalculation, Vancouver bypassed the mouth of the Columbia and left it for explorers from the United States to find.

A few days later and only a few miles up the coastline, Vancouver encountered the ship *Columbia,* captained by Robert Gray. A Boston merchant, Gray had frequented these waters for several years, trading with the Indians for luxurious sea otter pelts. On an earlier trip he had distinguished himself by becoming the first American sea captain to sail around the world. His current trading mission had so far proved successful, despite trouble with Haida Indians in the Queen Charlotte Islands.

Gray and Vancouver arranged to meet aboard one of their ships to discuss the mysterious river that Heceta had described. Gray admitted that he had tried to enter a likely looking inlet several weeks earlier, but to no avail. He also told Vancouver about an ocean inlet to the north, which Vancouver later explored and named Puget Sound after Peter Puget, a member of his crew. The two captains parted amicably.

On May 11, 1792, Gray made his monumental discovery and described it in his log.

> *At half past seven [p.m.], we were out clear of the bars and directed our course to the southward, along shore. . . . At four, a.m., saw the entrance of our desired port bearing east-south-east, distance six leagues. . . . At eight, a.m., being a little windward of the entrance of the Harbor, bore away, and run in east-north-east between the breakers, having from five to seven fathoms of water. When we were over the bar, we found this to be a large river of fresh water, up which we steered. . . . The entrance between the bars bore west-south-west, distant ten miles; the north side of the river a half mile distant from the ship; the south side of the same two and a half miles' distance.*

Gray christened the river Columbia in honor of his ship. He and his crew spent the next several days exploring the mouth of the great stream and trading with the friendly Indians. John Boit was a fifth mate aboard the *Columbia,* and he left the following account of the ship's encounter with the local people:

> *The beach was lin'd with Natives, who ran along shore following the Ship. Soon after above 20 Canoes came off, and brought a good lot of Furs and Salmon, which last they sold two for a board Nail. The furs we likewise bought cheap, for Copper and Cloth. They appear'd to view the Ship with greatest astonishment and no doubt we was the first civilized people that they*

> *ever saw. . . . at length we arriv'd opposite to a large village, situate on the North side of the river about 5 leagues from the entrance. . . . The river at this place was about 4 miles over. We purchas'd 4 Otter Skins for a Sheet of Copper, Beaver Skins, 2 Spikes each, and other land furs, 1 Spike each.*

Gray found that the forests lining the Columbia River were rich in game and that the people were anxious to trade. According to Boit,

> *The Indians are very numerous, and appear'd very civill (not even offering to steal). During our short stay we collected 150 Otter, 300 Beaver, and twice the Number of other land furs. The river abounds with excellent Salmon, and most other River fish, and the Woods with plenty of Moose and Dear, the skins of which was brought us in great plenty, and the Banks produces a ground Nut, which is an excellent substitute for either bread or Potatoes. We found plenty of Oak, Ash, and Walnut trees, and clear ground in plenty, which with little labour might be made fit to raise such seeds as is necessary for the sustenance of inhabitants.*

Gray and his crew had performed an important service for their country. Five decades later, when the United States and Great Britain would bicker over the placement of the boundary separating their realms, Gray's claim to the Columbia River would help ensure that Oregon Territory, including today's state of Washington, became part of the United States of America.

LEWIS AND CLARK REACH THE PACIFIC COAST

- 1805 -

On October 10, 1805, the explorers Meriwether Lewis and William Clark, along with their "Corps of Discovery," entered what would later become the state of Washington. The men had left St. Louis, Missouri, more than seventeen months earlier, and, after spending the winter of 1804–5 with the Mandan Indians in present-day North Dakota, had pushed on toward their goal of reaching the Pacific Ocean. A grueling and difficult journey had taken the expedition up the Missouri River to its headwaters. From there the party crossed the Bitterroot Mountains and then floated down today's Clearwater River to its confluence with the Snake River near the present-day Washington-Idaho border.

The Snake River presented the explorers with some special problems. "The river is as usual much obstructed by islands and rapids, some of which are difficult to pass," complained Captain Clark in his notes of the expedition. Rapids were everywhere on the turbulent river. Two days later Clark described more of their experiences on the Snake River.

> *At five miles we passed a rapid; at eight another rapid, and a small island on the right, and at ten and a half a small island on the right. We halted a mile and a half below for the purpose of examining a much larger and more dangerous rapid than those we had yet passed. It is three miles in length, and very difficult to navigate. We had scarcely set out, when three of the canoes stuck fast in endeavouring to avoid the rocks in the channel; soon after in passing two small rocky islands, one of the canoes struck a rock, but was prevented from upsetting, and fortunately we all arrived safe at the lower end of the rapid.*

More treacherous rapids followed, but on October 16, Lewis and Clark arrived at the confluence of the Snake and Columbia Rivers, near today's towns of Pasco and Kennewick. The party had traveled 3,714 miles from St. Louis. The next day, the men measured the two rivers and found the Columbia to be 960 yards wide at the junction. The Snake was 575 yards wide at its mouth. However, after the two giant rivers merged, the combined Columbia was estimated to range from one to three miles in width.

It was on such information, obtained by the Lewis and Clark expedition, that the U.S. scientific community relied for much of its early knowledge of the natural history and ethnology of the American West. Both captains were great observers and took copious notes. These were later translated into book form and published in two volumes in Philadelphia in 1814 under the formidable title *History of the Expedition Under the Command of Captains Lewis and Clark, to the Sources of the Missouri, thence Across the Rocky Mountains and Down the River Columbia to the Pacific Ocean.*

One curiosity reported in the *History* was the poor dental health exhibited by the Wanapum Indians, a Washington tribe related to the Nez Perce and called "Sokulks" by the captains.

> *Among the Sokulks too, and indeed among all the tribes whose chief subsistence is fish, we have observed that bad teeth are very general: some have the teeth, particularly those of the upper jaw, worn down to the gums, and many of both sexes, and even of middle age, have lost them almost entirely. This decay of the teeth is a circumstance very unusual among the Indians, either of the mountains or the plains, and seems peculiar to the inhabitants of the Columbia.*

The *History* also reported the two captains' theory regarding a peculiar eye disease suffered by many of the natives.

> *The fish [salmon] is, indeed, their chief food, except the roots, and the casual supplies of antelope. . . . This diet may be the direct or the remote cause of the chief disorder which prevails among them, as well as among the Flatheads, on the Kooskooskee and Lewis's river. With all these Indians a bad soreness of the eyes is a very common disorder, which is suffered to ripen by neglect, till many are deprived of one of their eyes, and some have totally lost the use of both. This dreadful calamity*

> *may reasonably, we think, be imputed to the constant reflection of the sun on the waters where they are constantly fishing in the spring, summer and fall, and during the rest of the year on the snows which affords no object to relieve the sight.*

Lewis and Clark and their weary followers continued down the Columbia River. On October 18 they sighted "a mountain to the S.W. the form of which is conical, and its top covered with snow." Most likely they had seen Mount Hood. On November 2 the expedition passed Beacon Rock, a huge monolith of stone that jutted over the Columbia on the Washington side of the river. It was here that the observant captains first noticed tidewater backing up the river from the Pacific.

A few days afterward the expedition approached the Pacific Ocean. "Great joy in camp we are in View of the Ocian," wrote Clark on November 7. Although the party was still a few miles from the Pacific itself, Clark was close enough to know that it couldn't be much farther. "This great pacific Octean which we been So long anxious to See. and the roeing or noise made by the waves brakeing on the rockey Shores (as I suppose) may be heard distinctly," continued Clark, who was not known for his spelling ability.

From November 10 until November 25, the crew camped along the Washington side of the Columbia. They explored as far as Cape Disappointment (Clark even hiked about nine miles north up the Pacific coast) before turning back upriver and crossing to its south side on November 26. After camping at present-day Port Williams, Oregon, from November 27 till December 7, the expedition moved to the site of Fort Clatsop and built winter camp. Its members stayed there until March 23, 1806, and then began their homeward journey.

LOST IN THE WILDERNESS

- 1812 -

Nineteen-year-old Ross Cox, an Irish-born clerk for John Jacob Astor's Pacific Fur Company, was lost! There was no doubt about it. When he awoke from an afternoon nap on a warm day in August 1812 and returned to the previous night's campsite, he discovered that all his companions had left without him. There he was in the wilds of present-day eastern Washington with no supplies, no equipment, no horse, and no weapons. Cox, in no way an experienced man of the wilderness, was terrified.

The likable Irish lad had left the Astoria post in June along with ninety-seven other men. Their mission was to forge up the mighty Columbia River, collect furs from the Indians along the way, and establish a new post on the Spokane River, a westward-flowing tributary of the Columbia. The party had run into difficulty almost immediately after leaving Astoria. Cox later detailed the experience in *Adventures on the Columbia River*, an account of his years as a fur trader: "We had half expected Indian trouble, but were totally unprepared for that overwhelming army of fleas that attacked on front, flank and rear. Our only defense was to strip off our clothes and dip them in the water, thus drowning the swarms of invaders."

After recovering from the flea attack and avoiding an encounter with Indians along the river, the party finally made its way to the mouth of the Walla Walla River. There its leaders met with a delegation of Walla Walla Indians, who, according to Cox, "were decidedly the most friendly we had met." The Astorians bought many horses from the tribe.

The group then traveled through Nez Perce country, and Cox left modern generations a detailed account of the tribe's lifestyle.

> *These Nez Perces (Pierced Noses) live in huts made of poles covered with mats of bark or rushes. Some houses were oblong, some cone-shaped, and some square. An opening at the top served the double purpose of window and chimney. They were clean, ambitious, smart-looking people who were fond of their children and kind to the aged. Apparently, they were all in good health, although many were afflicted with sore eyes. Both men and women wore a sort of leather shirt reaching to the knees. In addition, the men wore leggings made of some kind of skin. The Nez Perces were good hunters and excellent horsemen. Their saddles were made of dressed deerskin stuffed with hair. The wooden stirrups were covered with raw skin which, when dry, became hard and lasted a long time. Bridles were merely ropes made out of the hair from horses' tails.*

It was shortly after leaving the Nez Perce village that Cox was left behind. Dressed in only "a gingham shirt and summer trousers, badly worn moccasins, and no hat," the young trader was ill prepared for what faced him over the next fourteen days. When he returned to the campsite—just a few hundred yards from the forested dell to which he had wandered to pick cherries and take a nap—it was deserted. By then it was about five o'clock in the evening, and the coals from the fires indicated that his companions had probably left about three hours previously.

Cox camped nearby for the night, and early the next day he headed east in an attempt to catch up with his fellows. He saw two riders at a distance but was unable to attract their attention. The following night Cox was confronted by a giant rattlesnake but escaped unharmed. Trying to settle into a small cave the next night, Cox was surprised and terrified when a big gray wolf emerged from the cavern.

Days of wandering in the wilderness turned into a week. By then Cox's clothes were torn to shreds, his "moccasins were completely gone, and . . . feet were torn and bruised by thorns and sharp rocks." He lived off the land, eating wild cherries and berries when he could find them. Unarmed, he found it impossible to kill game to supplement his meager diet. In an encounter with a grizzly bear, Cox saved himself by climbing a tree. After waiting several hours for the bear to leave, he descended from his perch and escaped.

Finally, after two weeks of aimless wandering, Cox chanced upon an Indian camp. The friendly people fed and clothed him. The next day they escorted Cox to the Spokane River, where the other Astorians were building a fort near Spokane House, a post that belonged to the Pacific Fur Company's competitor, the North West Company. Cox described his reunion.

> *My deerskin robe and tanned complexion deceived them for a minute, but when they recognized me a great shout went up. All the men thronged around me, asking me questions, and congratulating me upon being found. I had been given up for lost. Just the day before, my clothing had been sold at auction, but now the purchasers hurried to bring it back to me. A holiday was declared to celebrate my return, and the Indians who had taken care of me were liberally rewarded.*

Cox left Fort Spokane the following May. When he arrived at Astoria, he learned that the United States and Great Britain were at war. In late October Astor's Pacific Fur Company sold Fort Astoria and all of its supplies and equipment to the Canadian-owned North West Company, and Cox became an employee of the new masters at Fort George, the new name given to Astoria.

Over the next several years, Cox traveled extensively between Fort George and the interior fur posts of the North West Company. In April 1816 he was placed in charge of the post at Fort Okanogan, which had been built in the summer of 1811 and was the first U.S. settlement in what is today the state of Washington.

In late 1816, although still a young man, Cox retired from his life as a fur trader and returned to Fort George. Then, on April 16, 1817, he began an overland journey that eventually carried him to Montreal. From there Cox returned to Dublin, married, and became a newspaper correspondent and a clerk for the Dublin Police Department.

Cox's later life remains a mystery. Neither his date of death nor place of burial is known. Fortunately for future generations, however, his valuable book, *Adventures on the Columbia River,* remains.

ALEXANDER ROSS AT FORT NEZ PERCES

- 1818 -

Pacific Fur Company clerk Alexander Ross was hard at work at the confluence of the Okanogan and Columbia Rivers, near the present-day towns of Brewster and Bridgeport. Ross's superiors at Fort Astoria had sent him to build a fort and fur-trading post at the critical junction of the rivers. Arriving there in early September 1811, Ross and his party erected a sixteen-by-twenty-foot long log house, one of the first U.S. structures in today's state of Washington. The men called the place Okanogan Post, and Ross was left in charge.

Ross was born in 1783 in Scotland. At age twenty-one he had left his family and sailed to Canada, where he taught school. Some years later he heard of John Jacob Astor's forming of the Pacific Fur Company, and in 1810 he joined the fledgling concern. In September Ross, along with several new company recruits, left New York City aboard a ship called the *Tonquin.* Upon arriving at the mouth of the

Columbia River in March 1811, the party started work on Fort Astoria, the proposed hub of Astor's western fur-trading empire.

Soon Ross departed for Okanogan on his fort-building mission. As clerk-in-charge of the new post, He spent most of the winter of 1811–12 alone at Okanogan Post. His success at the post—trading for more than fifteen hundred beaver pelts during a six-month period—assured him several more years as manager there. When Astor's fur interests were sold to the North West Company in 1813, Ross stayed on board with the new management. He was transferred back to Fort George (formerly Astoria) in 1816.

In 1817 Ross left Fort George and was sent to a post on the Thompson River in Canada. From there he traveled to the Walla Walla region, where he assisted in the construction of a new fur station to be named Fort Nez Perces. The new fort, located on the Columbia River, was to become the central supply depot for all the rest of the North West Company's interior posts, replacing Spokane House, which the company had built a few years earlier at the junction of the Spokane and Little Spokane Rivers. The company management had decided that the new site was more centrally located for both North West Company trading parties and the various Indian tribes with whom they traded.

The construction crew arrived at the Walla Walla site in July 1818 and began work immediately. In his book *The Fur Hunters of the Far West,* Ross gave a vivid description of the problems in building the post.

> *We were in an unfriendly land with a gigantic task on our hands. In the whole country, this spot was the hardest! Nevertheless the region had to be made safe for the fur trade, the friendship of the natives secured,*

> *buildings made, furs collected, and new territories added. This was a big program, and we did not dare see obstacles ahead. Our orders were to occupy the position, so on the dreaded spot we took our stand to run every risk, and brave every danger.*

Indeed, the construction of Fort Nez Perces was a big undertaking. According to Ross the site was a "commanding one." The Columbia River guarded it on the west. To the north and east "stretched a wide expanse of never-ending plains." And to the south the foothills of the Blue Mountains protected the location.

Built along the same lines of other fur posts in the region, the "Gibraltar of the Columbia," as Ross called it, "rose proudly above the mighty river, a symbol of the white man's power in the land of the red man." Ross carefully described Fort Nez Perces in his book.

> *The whole establishment was surrounded by a palisade made of ponderous planks of timber twenty feet long, two and a half feet broad, and six inches thick. The outside of this wall was made very smooth to keep the enemy from climbing it. Built on the top of the palisade was a range of balustrades four feet high which served the double purpose of ramparts and loopholes, (a protecting wall made of planks put close together in the form of a railing). On the inside, a strong gallery five feet wide, extended all around. Sentinels on guard paced back and forth along this gallery . . . At each corner, where a strong bastion or blockhouse was built, was a reservoir that held two hundred gallons of water*

> *as a security against fire, the thing we dreaded most in the plots of natives. Inside the wall were built ranges of storehouses, and cabins for the hands. In front of these buildings was another wall twelve feet high, with port-holes and slip doors, which separated the buildings from the open square inside. . . . The outer gate was cleverly made to open and shut by a pulley, and two double doors secured the entrance.*

The weapons that protected Fort Nez Perces were formidable for the time. The armament consisted of four cannons, ten swivel guns, sixty muskets, twenty pikes, and a box of hand grenades. And, just to be safe and to protect the fort from illegal entry, as Ross recalled, "all trading was done through a hole in the wall of the trading shop, we standing on the inside, and the natives on the outside."

Ross stayed on as the manager of Fort Nez Perces until 1822, when he elected to leave the employment of what was now the Hudson's Bay Company (the previous year Hudson's Bay had merged with the North West Company). However, the company persuaded him to stay on for another year to take command of a fur brigade bound for the Snake River country. After conscientiously serving three different fur companies, Ross finally retired to the present-day city of Winnipeg, Manitoba, where the Hudson's Bay Company gave him a one-hundred-acre land grant. There he became superintendent of schools, pursued his writing interests, and died in 1856.

THE CHRISTENING OF FORT VANCOUVER

- 1825 -

On a chilly Saturday morning, March 19, 1825, a small crowd of interested onlookers gathered in a courtyard to watch the erection of a flagpole. Some important people were there, including George Simpson, the governor of the Northern Department of the huge Hudson's Bay Company. Simpson had journeyed 2,900 miles to survey his company's posts in the Oregon country and to help establish a new one. On this occasion he had brought with him Dr. John McLoughlin, the new chief agent for the company's operations in the Pacific Northwest.

The new post was Fort Vancouver, and it was located on the northern bank of the Columbia River about one hundred miles upstream from the Pacific Ocean. The fort was the property of the Hudson's Bay Company and was designed to be the new primary supply depot for all the other company forts scattered throughout the Northwest wilderness. Fort Vancouver was to replace Fort George—

the former U.S. post called Astoria, located on the opposite bank of the Columbia near its mouth in present-day Oregon. Then, in the event the river ever became the boundary line between the United States and Canada, the new fort would be on the British side. The site for the new fort had been selected by McLoughlin and his predecessor, Alexander Kennedy, only a few days after McLoughlin arrived at Fort George the previous fall.

Simpson, McLoughlin, and the crowd of Indians, English, and Scottish trappers, Hawaiian Island laborers, and French-Canadian voyageurs watched as the flagpole was hoisted into place. Then the Hudson's Bay Company flag was run up the staff, and Governor Simpson christened the pole with a bottle of rum. The dedication signified that the giant British-run Hudson's Bay Company intended to continue and even enlarge its northwestern field of operations. At the same time, Fort Vancouver had been constructed on the Columbia River's northern bank to give notice to the United States that, if ever the two powers decided on a permanent border, it would be one that relinquished no British territory north of the Columbia River.

After christening the flagstaff, Governor Simpson stepped forward and spoke a few words: "In behalf of the Honourable Hudson's Bay Company I hereby name this establishment Fort Vancouver. God save King George the fourth." In a letter to his company's board of directors in London, Simpson elaborated upon his choice of designations for the fort, even though he knew his logic was historically incorrect and that it was the American captain Robert Gray who had really rediscovered and claimed the Columbia River. Nevertheless, Simpson wrote, "The object of naming it after that distinguished navigator [Captain George Vancouver], is to identify our Soil and Trade with his discovery of the River and Coast on behalf of Great Britain."

McLoughlin was a shrewd and capable administrator, and under his direction Fort Vancouver thrived. McLoughlin was born in Canada in 1784 and at age eighteen obtained his license "to Practice in surgery and Pharmacy or as an Apothecary." He immediately hired on with the North West Company as an assistant physician. He later moved into the administrative end of the company's business and was placed in charge of several fur posts in central Canada.

When the North West and Hudson's Bay Companies merged in 1821, McLoughlin remained with the fort. His success in competing with rival American fur traders along the international border did not escape the attention of his superiors, and when it came time to select the best agent for the Pacific Northwest, McLoughlin was an easy choice. In 1829 Governor Simpson noted McLoughlin's success. The governor commended McLoughlin, saying that his management was "conspicuous for a talent in planning and for an activity and perseverance in execution which reflects highest credit on your judgment and habits of business."

Construction of a new Fort Vancouver began in 1829. Located a little less than a mile downstream from the original, this fort was much bigger in order to accommodate the fur post's increased activity. Enlarged in 1835, the second fort eventually evolved into a gigantic stockade just a bit smaller than five modern-day football fields placed side by side.

Beginning in 1843 with the opening of the Oregon Trail, thousands of American settlers arrived in Oregon Territory. Although the border dispute between Great Britain and the United States was still unsettled, McLoughlin treated all newcomers with kindness, politeness, and, if needed, assistance. In time his British superiors tired of the kindly doctor's hospitality toward Americans. He was eventually demoted and, more or less, forced to retire. He and his family then moved across the Columbia River to Oregon City, where he became an American citizen.

By 1846, when the Oregon boundary dispute between Great Britain and the United States was finally resolved, Fort Vancouver was officially on U.S. territory. However, for several years the British continued to operate the fort, which by that time had lost a great deal of its importance due to the rapid decline of the fur trade. Beginning in 1849 the U.S. Army finally took over the site and, a few hundred yards north of the old fort, established Camp Columbia—later called Columbia Barracks, and later still, Fort Vancouver Military Reservation.

Today one can visit a partial reconstruction of the Hudson's Bay Company's Fort Vancouver as it existed during its heyday in the 1840s. Located within the city limits of Vancouver, Washington, on the exact site of the second fort, today's version provides a living history lesson of that important period of American history when two great nations vied for the lucrative fur trade of the Pacific Northwest.

THE UNITED STATES EXPLORING EXPEDITION

- 1841 -

AT SIX O'CLOCK IN THE MORNING ON WEDNESDAY, APRIL 28, 1841, the USS *Vincennes,* a seven-hundred-ton sloop of war carrying approximately 190 crew members, approached the craggy coast at Cape Disappointment. Twenty-two days out of the Hawaiian Islands, the *Vincennes* now planned to explore the shorelines of today's states of Washington, Oregon, and California. The coastal survey was part of a four-year expedition that started in 1838 and was called the U.S. Exploring Expedition, or more commonly, the Wilkes Expedition, after its leader, Lieutenant Charles Wilkes.

The U.S. Exploring Expedition had a broad mission of science. Plans for such an expedition had been made years earlier, but it was not until August 18, 1838, that the expedition actually got under way. On that day the *Vincennes,* accompanied by five other navy ships—*Peacock, Flying Fish, Relief, Porpoise,* and *Sea Gull*—sailed out of Hampton Roads, Virginia, on a worldwide journey.

Although thirty-eight of the forty lieutenants reporting for active service had logged more sea duty than Lieutenant Wilkes, he was chosen for command because, as one modern-day historian, Herman J. Viola, claimed, "He had the vision, intelligence, and determination to do the job." Wilkes turned out to be an excellent choice. In America's first attempt to combine the talents of civilian scientists and navy support personnel, Wilkes succeeded grandly. When the expedition returned to the United States on June 10, 1842, it had surveyed all areas of the globe and collected tens of thousands of natural history and ethnological specimens that eventually became the foundation for the Smithsonian Institution's National Museum of Natural History.

From Cape Disappointment the *Vincennes* made its way up the Pacific coast, reaching the Strait of Juan de Fuca on May 1. On May 7 it arrived at what is today known as Port Townsend, at the entrance to Puget Sound. Four days later, at Fort Nisqually, a Hudson's Bay Company post at the south end of Puget Sound, Lieutenant Wilkes and some members of the expedition left the *Vincennes* for a month-long exploration of the interior. Before leaving, however, Wilkes sent Lieutenant Robert E. Johnson on an exploring mission across the Cascade Mountains all the way to the Columbia River near Spokane.

In the Spokane area Lieutenant Johnson heard an Indian story that is one of the earliest references to Mount St. Helens and its destructive forces. The story of the 1800 eruption of Mount St. Helens was told by an old chief sometimes called Cornelius. The Wilkes expedition's geologist, James Dwight Dana, later recorded the tale.

> *Cornelius, when about ten years of age, was sleeping in a lodge with a great many people, and was suddenly awakened by his mother, who called out to him that*

> *the world was falling to pieces. He then heard a great noise of thunder overhead, and all the people crying out in terror. Something was falling very thick, which they at first took for snow, but on going out they found it to be dirt: it proved to be ashes, which fell to the depth of six inches, and increased their fears, by causing them to suppose that the end of the world was actually at hand.*

Wilkes's own scientific wanderings carried him to Fort Vancouver. From there he sent parties to reconnoiter the Willamette River valley of Oregon and the overland route to San Francisco.

Although the U.S. Exploring Expedition's official mission was purely scientific, Wilkes's personal agenda in the Pacific Northwest included observation and the gathering of data that could be useful to U.S. authorities in their dealings with Great Britain over the Oregon boundary dispute. At Fort Nisqually, for example, he sent a letter to the secretary of the navy.

> *I shall continue my operations in the waters of this Territory and keep parties engaged in the interior during the time we remain; obtaining as much knowledge of the country as possible, being well aware of the importance of accurate information for the use of the government relative to the value of the country, pending the settlement of the boundary question.*

Indeed, the geographical knowledge gained from Wilkes's overland reconnaissance and the maps the expedition produced as a result were of paramount importance to the United States a few years later when the boundary line between Oregon Territory and Canada was finally negotiated with Great Britain.

All was not perfect on the well-orchestrated expedition, however. At the mouth of the Columbia River, in mid-July 1841, the *Peacock* ran aground and was destroyed, along with all the valuable natural history specimens and notes that were aboard. Wilkes, however, was pleased and impressed by the hospitality shown by Dr. John McLoughlin and his Hudson's Bay Company employees at Fort Vancouver during the crisis. The company provided the men with food and shelter until another ship was purchased and outfitted.

After replacing the lost *Peacock* with the new ship *Oregon,* the U.S. Exploring Expedition departed the Pacific Northwest bound for San Francisco. From California the ships sailed back to the Hawaiian Islands, then to the Philippines and Singapore, around the Cape of Good Hope, and finally across the Atlantic Ocean to New York.

The success of the Wilkes expedition was overwhelming. Hundreds of new species of plants and animals were brought back to the United States for study, and the maps and charts of theretofore unknown regions of the globe provided geographers with a gold mine of knowledge. Antarctica was determined to be a stand-alone continent, nearly three hundred Pacific islands were charted, and the coastline of the Pacific Northwest was explored as it had never been before.

Lieutenant Wilkes personally supervised the publication of the findings of his expedition. The results, *Narrative of the United States Exploring Expedition During the Years 1838, 1839, 1840, 1841, 1842,* was published as a five-volume set in 1845. Wilkes himself eventually rose to the rank of rear admiral, although he was retired at the time. He died in February 1877 in Washington, D.C., and his remains rest at Arlington National Cemetery.

EXPLORING WASHINGTON WITH JOHN C. FRÉMONT

- 1843 -

On October 22, 1843, the noted American explorer John Charles Frémont entered what is today the state of Washington. With him on his second expedition to the far American West were his topographer, Charles Preuss; famed mountain man Thomas Fitzpatrick (serving as guide); Christopher "Kit" Carson; and several other American, Creole, and French-Canadian adventurers. The exploring party left Missouri on May 17 and made its way across the Great Plains to the Rocky Mountains. The men crossed South Pass and visited the Great Salt Lake. Then they made their way north to Fort Boise and beyond, into the Oregon country.

The previous year Frémont and another party had journeyed on the future Oregon Trail from Independence, Missouri, up the Platte River, and finally to the Continental Divide of the Rocky Mountains before returning to Missouri and preparing for the second, longer expedition. From the Oregon country Frémont's travels would carry him beyond Washington to the Great Basin of Nevada, through California, across the Mojave Desert, and back to Missouri across the southern Great Plains.

As Lieutenant Frémont and his exploring party crossed from present-day Oregon into Washington on that autumn day in 1843, he described the scene in his journal.

> *The white frost this morning was like snow on the ground; the ice was a quarter of an inch thick on the creek, and the thermometer at sunrise was at 20°. But, in a few hours, the day became warm and pleasant, and our road over the mountains was delightful and full of enjoyment. . . . On our right was a mountain plateau, covered with a dense forest; and to the westward, immediately below us, was the great Nez Perce (pierced nose) prairie, in which dark lines of timber indicated the course of many affluents to a considerable stream that was seen pursuing its way across the plain towards what appeared to be the Columbia river. This I knew to be the Walahwalah [Walla Walla] river.*

Frémont and his men then descended to the Columbia River, passing through a forest of "*hemlock* spruce" containing trees with circumferences of 10 to 12 feet and standing 110 feet high. In the afternoon, just before reaching the Walla Walla River, Frémont spied Mount Hood "standing high out above the surrounding country, at the distance of 180 miles." With a sunset temperature of 48 degrees Fahrenheit, the expedition prepared to bed down for the night.

On October 24 Lieutenant Frémont's party reached the missionary station of Dr. Marcus Whitman. Whitman and his wife, Narcissa, had left a comfortable life in the East to settle among the Indians and to minister to them at a little outpost located almost thirty miles east of Fort Walla Walla. Dr. Whitman was absent that day, but Frémont recorded in his journal that he "had the pleasure to see a fine-looking large family of emigrants, men, women, and children, in robust health."

The following day Frémont's party arrived at Fort Walla Walla, the Hudson's Bay Company fur post located at the junction of the Walla Walla and Columbia Rivers. The mighty Columbia did not escape Frémont's attention, or awe: "We here saw, for the first time, the great river on which the course of events for the last half century has been directing attention and conferring historical fame. The river is, indeed, a noble object, and has here attained its full magnitude."

The expedition left Fort Walla Walla on October 28, following the mighty Columbia down its eastern bank. It soon crossed the border back into present-day Oregon and stayed in that state until the travelers reached The Dalles. There, Frémont wrote, "our land journey found . . . its western termination." Thinking that ferrying across the wide river and blazing a trail through the thick Washington wilderness to Fort Vancouver would be too much trouble, Frémont decided to mark the spot as the beginning of the homeward journey. He left some of the group to prepare for the long trip home while he floated downriver in a borrowed Indian canoe to Fort Vancouver, where he intended to purchase supplies for the return trip to Missouri.

When he reached Fort Vancouver a couple of days later, Frémont was met by the indomitable Dr. John McLoughlin, who received him "with the courtesy and hospitality for which he has been eminently distinguished, and which makes a forcible and delightful impression on a traveler from the long wilderness from which we had issued." After resupplying from the vast stores of Fort Vancouver, Frémont departed on November 10 and directed his tiny command of twenty men, along with a barge and three canoes full of equipment, back up the Columbia. They arrived at The Dalles eight days later.

On November 25, 1843, Lieutenant Frémont and his party of explorers left the banks of the Columbia on their southward journey home. Somewhere along the way plans were changed. Instead of dropping southeast to the headwaters of the Arkansas River, then eastward toward home, the expedition ended up wandering all over the Great Basin, across the Sierra Nevada to Sutter's Fort in California, through the deserts of the extreme Southwest, and finally, by a circuitous route, across the Rockies and the southern Great Plains. Frémont finally reached St. Louis on August 6 of the following year.

During his two expeditions of 1842 and 1843–44, Frémont mapped much of the future Oregon Trail between the Missouri frontier and Fort Vancouver. In a later expedition he returned to California and participated actively in the so-called Bear Flag Rebellion. In 1856 he became the first presidential nominee for the newly organized Republican Party but lost the election to the Democrat James Buchanan. During the Civil War he served as a general in the U.S. Army, and later he served several years as governor of the Arizona Territory. He died virtually penniless in New York City in 1890.

"FIFTY-FOUR FORTY OR FIGHT"

- 1846 -

Jesse Looney, a recent arrival in the Oregon country, wrote a letter to those back home in Missouri. It was October 27, 1843, and Looney wrote from Dr. Marcus Whitman's mission on the Walla Walla River.

> *The company of emigrants came through safely this season to the number of a thousand persons with something over a hundred wagons to this place . . . and, with the exception of myself, and a few others, have all gone on down [to the Willamette Valley]. . . . There were five or six deaths on the road . . . and there were some eight or ten births. Upon the whole we fared better than we expected.*

The emigrant party that Looney referred to in his letter was the one sometimes called the Great Emigration of 1843. Consisting of about eight hundred men, women, and children [Looney overestimated the number] and 110 wagons, as well as three thousand mules, horses, oxen, and cattle, this was the first large party to travel the newly laid-out Oregon Trail from the Missouri frontier to the western reaches of Oregon. Following the pioneers of the "Great Emigration," tens of thousands of families journeyed along the trail in search of new lives in the lands of Oregon and California.

Oregon, which at the time included what are today the states of Washington, Idaho, and Oregon, as well as parts of Montana, Wyoming, and British Columbia, had for years been a treasure house for both British and American fur interests. John Jacob Astor's Pacific Fur Company had established a U.S. presence as early as 1811 at the mouth of the Columbia River. Astor's men were closely followed by traders of the North West Company, who commandeered Astoria for the British during the War of 1812.

No agreement had ever been reached about the exact location of the border between the United States and Canada, and both Great Britain and the United States claimed Oregon, or at least large parts of it. The continual arrival of thousands of American families over the Oregon Trail, however, suddenly cast a different light on the issue. It soon became desirable, from the U.S. standpoint at least, to settle the boundary issue once and for all. Although most people agreed that a boundary line must be settled on by the two countries, there were those who felt the land was useless—Senator Thomas Hart Benton once proclaimed that he "wouldn't accept Vancouver Island as a present," and a prominent British foreign minister called Oregon "a mere pine swamp."

While the feeling in Washington, D.C., was that the dividing line should fall on the latitude of 54°40' north, British authorities preferred a line farther south, giving Canada considerably more territory. By the time the new U.S. president, James K. Polk, an admitted expansionist, took office in March 1845, Americans were anxious for a settlement. The slogan "Fifty-four forty or fight!" was the motto of the day, fueled in part by President Polk himself. Polk asserted his position on the border issue at his inauguration.

> *Nor will it become in a less degree my duty to assert and maintain by all constitutional means the right of the United States to that portion of our territory which lies beyond the Rocky Mountains. Our title to the country of Oregon is "clear and unquestionable," and already are our people preparing to perfect that title by occupying it with their wives and children.*

Perhaps the British were a little taken aback by the otherwise mild-mannered Polk's pronouncements on the Oregon issue. Although it was obvious that the United States was about to get involved in a war with Mexico, Polk didn't back off from the Oregon dispute. He told James Buchanan, his secretary of state, that he could handle two wars if necessary: "I would meet the war [with] England . . . and stand and fight until the last man among us fell in conflict. . . . Neither as citizen or President would I permit or tolerate any intermeddling of any European Power on this continent."

In any event, in 1845 the British-controlled Hudson's Bay Company moved its hub of operations from Fort Vancouver on the north bank of the Columbia River to Fort Victoria on Vancouver Island, considerably farther north, but still south of the forty-ninth parallel, a boundary line that the United States had advocated for years prior to the "Fifty-Four Forty or Fight" campaign.

Finally, the British statesman Lord Aberdeen (George Hamilton-Gordon) told Parliament, "My lords, I consider war to be the greatest folly, if not the greatest crime of which a country could be guilty, if lightly entered into." Aberdeen then submitted a compromise for the settlement of the Oregon boundary to the United States. The compromise called for the existing boundary line that separated the United States and Canada from Lake of the Woods (Minnesota) to the Rocky Mountains—that is, the forty-ninth parallel—to be extended to the Pacific coast, with the exception of Vancouver Island. Both countries would be left with an outlet to the sea, and Vancouver Island would belong to Canada.

President Polk was pleased with the proposal and submitted it to the U.S. Senate. It was approved on June 12, 1846, and made official on August 5 of that same year. The United States finally had a permanent boundary between itself and Canada, from the Atlantic to the Pacific.

THE WHITMAN MASSACRE

- 1847 -

It was May 1844, at Waiilatpu Mission, located near Fort Walla Walla. Dr. Marcus Whitman wrote a letter to the parents of his wife, Narcissa, who were back east. The epistle read in part:

> *I have no doubt our greatest work is to be to aid the white settlement of this Country & help to found its religious institutions. Providence has its full share in all these events. Although the Indians have made and are making rapid advances in Religious knowledge & civilization yet it cannot be hoped that time will be allowed to mature either the work of Christianization or Civilization before the White settlers will demand the soil and seek the removal of both the Indians & the Mission. What Americans desire of this kind they always effect and it is equally useless to oppose or desire it otherwise.*

Whitman prophesied the future when he wrote those words. Only a few years would pass before the white presence throughout the American West would become so dominant that tribes of native people would be forcibly removed from their homelands. It had already happened in the East when the Cherokees and other peaceable tribes were moved to strange lands beyond the Mississippi River. Whitman knew that the same thing would inevitably happen in the Pacific Northwest.

Ironically, however, it was not the white man who put an end to Whitman's religious crusade among the Indians of present-day Washington, Oregon, and Idaho. It was the Indians themselves. Members of the Cayuse tribe attacked Whitman's mission at Waiilatpu on November 29, 1847.

The circumstances that caused the Cayuse people to rise up and kill the Whitmans that fall day of 1847 are complex. A measles epidemic had recently visited the Indians, and perhaps they failed to understand why Whitman, a man of medicine, could not stop the dying. The Indians were the recipients of a plethora of diseases spread by the newly arriving whites, for which the native people had no immunity. They may have wondered why the white people Whitman attended always recovered, while many of the Indians, treated for the same diseases, didn't. It was Cayuse custom to kill shamans, or medicine men, who abused their healing power. Admiration and respect for the Whitmans turned to fear and hate, and the Cayuses fell upon the mission with a deadly purpose. In all, fourteen people were killed and forty-seven more taken prisoner.

Marcus and Narcissa Whitman had journeyed to the vast wilderness of the American West eleven years earlier, sent by the American Board of Commissioners for Foreign Missions, a group that represented Dutch Reformed Lutheran, Presbyterian, and Congregational churches. Along with a companion, Eliza Spalding, Narcissa became one of the first two white women to cross the Rocky Mountains. The Whitmans had married just before their departure from the East when they learned that only married couples would be sponsored by the American Board.

The Whitmans were eager to work with the Indians and to offer them Christianity and the benefits the doctor and his wife felt went with it. Marcus once wrote:

> *It gives me much pleasure to . . . quietly . . . work . . . for the Indians. It does not concern me so much what is to become of any particular set of Indians as to give them the offer of Salvation through the gospel & the opportunity of Civilization and then I am content to do good to all men as "I have opportunity."*

The Whitmans worked hard at their new professions, and the mission station at Waiilatpu was soon well-known among the various Indian tribes that inhabited the middle Columbia River valley. Marcus journeyed back east in 1842 to take care of mission business, and when he returned to Waiilatpu in the summer of 1843, he helped guide the wagons of the "Great Emigration," the first sizable wagon train to follow the newly charted Oregon Trail.

Soon after his return home, Marcus's mission station became a regular stopping-over place on the Oregon Trail. Since Marcus was trained as a physician, his medical skills were often solicited by the hundreds of emigrant families who arrived at the mission after traveling from the Missouri settlements. But Whitman did not limit his medical practice to the emigrants. With equal enthusiasm he set out to treat any and all arrivals to his mission.

Whitman's nephew visited the grisly remains of Waiilatpu Mission the year after the massacre. He later described the scene.

> *We found everything swept from the site of the mission, the buildings burned and everything in ruins. The bodies had been buried, but coyotes had dug into the graves considerable. I found what I satisfied myself was the Doctor's skull. There were two hatchet marks in the back of the head.*

Today the scene of the Whitman Massacre is a national historic site. Located six miles west of Walla Walla, it is a grim reminder of one of the first efforts to bring the white man's salvation to native people of the Pacific Northwest.

THE GREAT RAILROAD SURVEY

- 1853 -

IN EARLY 1853 NATIONAL ATTENTION WAS FOCUSED on the region that in March of the same year had become Washington Territory. One of the most pressing issues facing the westward-looking U.S. government was where to route a transcontinental railroad. The nation's citizens were divided over the railroad debate. In Congress proponents and politicians from both the North and the South tried to outtalk and outmaneuver their neighbors in getting the railroad route to run through their regions.

At the center of the controversy were two well-known men: Jefferson Davis, the U.S. secretary of war, and Thomas Hart Benton, a former senator from Missouri. Several alternative routes from the Mississippi River to the Pacific coast had already been proposed. Naturally Davis, a southerner, preferred one that traversed the southern sections of the country. Benton scoffed at the idea of running a railroad through the arid Southwest, saying that the terrain was "so utterly desolate, desert, and God-forsaken that Kit Carson says a wolf could not make a living on it." Benton's preference was the route that followed the thirty-eighth parallel from central Missouri to the Pacific Ocean.

Each of the proposed routes was promoted by its own regional advocates. Because there were so many different opinions about which route would be best for the railroad and for those in its path, Congress debated the matter for years before coming up with a scheme to solve the dilemma.

Congress passed legislation on March 2, 1853—the same day that President Millard Fillmore authorized the creation of Washington Territory—that gave Secretary of War Davis a practically impossible mission. Davis was instructed to provide Congress with detailed reports, supported by actual field surveys, of all the many proposed routes to the Pacific—within ten months!

Davis quickly mobilized the Corps of Topographical Engineers and sent a series of surveying parties into the western wilds to reconnoiter the several routes. The man chosen to head up the route between the forty-seventh and forty-ninth parallels, through Washington Territory, was Isaac I. Stevens. At the same time that he was appointed to this post, he was also made governor of the newly created territory.

Stevens was an 1839 West Point graduate and an engineer officer in the Coast Survey before he resigned to become the territorial governor. He attacked his new duties with the determination and vigor for which he was known. Stevens selected Captain George B. McClellan for his assistant. McClellan later became general in chief of all Union forces during the Civil War.

Governor Stevens wrote his own orders for the Pacific Railroad Survey. He was to

> *examine the passes of the several mountain ranges, the geography and meteorology of the whole intermediate*

> *region, the character, as avenues of trade and transportation, of the Missouri and Columbia rivers, the rains and snows of the route, especially in the mountain passes, and in short to collect every species of information bearing upon the question of railroad practicability . . . moreover to give great attention to the Indian tribes, as their friendship was important and bore directly upon the question both of the Pacific railroad and the safety of [the] party.*

Stevens proceeded on his survey, leaving St. Paul, Minnesota, on June 6, 1853. His route was to traverse the present-day states of North Dakota, Montana, Idaho, and Washington, ending up first at Fort Vancouver, then eventually at Puget Sound. Although Governor Stevens reported favorably on the northern route as a prime prospect for the transcontinental railroad, Dr. George Suckley, the naturalist on Stevens's survey party, was of a different opinion.

> *A road* might *be built over the tops of the Himalayeh [*sic*] mountains—but no reasonable man would undertake it. I think the same of the Northern route. Tunnels of two miles in length are not our only obstacles; gullies, steep grades and deep cuts are bad enough, but the almost innumerable heavy and strong bridges required, and the large number of short and sudden curves, frequently of less than 1,000 feet radius, are very serious obstacles.*

It seems that Suckley held the opinion of the majority. As it turned out, Stevens's report and recommendation for a northern railway route between the forty-seventh and forty-ninth parallels were looked upon dimly by engineering authorities.

Despite the mammoth expense of mounting multiple survey parties to map various railroad routes to the Pacific, when all the results were in (late, as might have been expected), nobody paid attention to the engineers' reports. Davis anticipated the end result of the surveys when, in 1858, he commented to the Congress,

> *With all due respect to my associates, I must say the location of this road will be a political question. It should be a question of engineering, a commercial question, a governmental question—not a question of partisan advantage or of sectional success in a struggle between parties and sections.*

Historian William H. Goetzmann, in his classic study of the U.S. Army Corps of Topographical Engineers, *Army Exploration in the American West 1803–1863,* writes, "Because of miscalculations in their conception, execution, and evaluation, the surveys in fact ultimately became the final stroke of doom to any plan for a federally sponsored transcontinental railroad before the Civil War."

Although the surveys had little bearing on the eventual routing of the first transcontinental railroad, they more than made up for it by the vast amount of biological, geological, and ethnological data they brought back with them. In fact, this information about relatively unknown regions provided scientists and ethnographers with a storehouse of information that kept them working for years.

GRANT'S LIFE AT FORT VANCOUVER

- 1853 -

The spring of 1853 found thirty-one-year-old Captain Sam Grant (eventually known to most as Ulysses S. Grant) more interested in his garden than he was in his military duties at Fort Vancouver, in the newly formed territory of Washington. There was little action at Vancouver, and Grant was looking forward to sending for his wife and young son to join him at the remote post on the Columbia River. On this warm May day, as he dug into the rich, damp earth, he carefully dropped seeds into place and hoped that, by autumn, he would be reunited with his family and have a nice harvest to place before his wife and child.

Delia B. Sheffield, a young woman who lived with her husband at Ford Vancouver, described Grant as he struggled in his garden.

> *Captains Grant and Wallin leased a tract of land from Mr. W. Nye, situated about a mile from the post, along the Columbia River, intending to raise a crop of potatoes*

on part of it, and seed the remainder to oats. The two officers ploughed the ground and planted that portion of it nearest the river with potatoes.

Passing this field one day, in the early spring, I saw Captain Grant, with his trousers tucked in his boots, sowing oats broadcast from a sheet tied about his neck and shoulders. Captain Grant worked thus in the hope of realizing a profit from his crop which would enable him to bring his wife and family out to live with him. His pay as Captain was not sufficient to meet his own expenses, and this was the cause of the farming venture. It was, however, a sad failure; the river overflowed and killed most of their potatoes.

Fort Vancouver was built by traders of Britain's Hudson's Bay Company in 1824–25. For years it had served as headquarters for the company's far-reaching fur-trading empire in the Pacific Northwest. However, the boundary dispute between Canada and the United States was finally resolved in 1846, and in May 1849 the Oregon Territory was officially claimed as a U.S. territory by Captain John S. Hatheway and two companies of the First U.S. Artillery.

The U.S. Army occupied Fort Vancouver in 1849. Relations between army personnel and remnants of the Hudson's Bay Company traders remained cordial, and the Hudson's Bay employees continued to work out of the fort for several more years until leaving for good in 1860. In the meantime soldiers had built barracks several hundred yards north of the original fort and christened the U.S. post Columbia Barracks. The name reverted to Fort Vancouver in July 1853.

Fort Vancouver in those days was not the most desirable place to live. Delia Sheffield wrote her thoughts upon her arrival at the post, probably in 1852.

> *My first impression of Vancouver was a dreary one and a feeling of homesickness came over me as I saw only a few old dilapidated log huts inhabited by half-breeds. But when we reached the garrison and I had a good view of the grand old Columbia River and the snow-clad peaks of Mt. St. Helens, Mt. Adams, and Mt. Hood, looking like giant sentries, I felt as if I could battle with the pioneer life of a new country.*
>
> *Life at Vancouver in 1852 and for several years later was of a very simple and primitive sort. Luxuries were not to be had and the necessaries of life were costly; eggs cost a dollar and a half a dozen, potatoes nine dollars a sack, and flour twenty-four dollars a barrel. Carpets were unobtainable, all furniture was rude and home-made, and fortunate were those who could secure pieces of furniture that had been brought across the plains, or around by the Isthmus.*

Grant had arrived at Fort Vancouver in 1852. The location of the secluded post, far removed from civilization, prompted him to leave his small family behind. But Grant had some good companions while at Fort Vancouver. One of his best friends was Captain George B. McClellan, a twenty-seven-year-old West Point graduate from Pennsylvania. Less than a decade later, both men would, at different times, be named general in chief of all Union armies during the Civil War.

Born near Cincinnati, Ohio, in 1822, Grant graduated from West Point in 1843, ranking about midway in his class. Hoping for a cavalry assignment, he was instead placed in an infantry unit and sent to St. Louis. After seeing action in the Mexican War, he served at various army posts in New York and Michigan, and finally at Fort Vancouver.

A despondent Grant left the army shortly after he was reassigned from Fort Vancouver. For seven years he worked in Missouri and Illinois as a firewood salesman, real estate agent, bill collector, and clerk in a tannery. Finally, in 1861, after the beginning of the Civil War and with the aid of the Illinois governor and a congressman, Grant was commissioned as a colonel of the Twenty-first Illinois Infantry. Two months later he was promoted to brigadier general of volunteers.

Although his first battle against the Confederate army—at Belmont, Missouri—nearly ended in disaster, Grant clearly demonstrated a knack for leadership. Belmont was followed by victories at Forts Henry and Donelson, at Shiloh, and at Lookout Mountain, all in Tennessee. Grant's brilliance as a commander soon earned his recall to Washington, D.C., where President Abraham Lincoln bestowed upon him the rank of lieutenant general and the position of general in chief of all U.S. armies.

After the war, in 1868, Grant was elected eighteenth president of the United States, the first of several Union generals to be so honored. From the East Portico of the Capitol on March 4, 1869, the captain-gardener once stationed at Fort Vancouver made a promise to the American people: "The office has come to me unsought; I commence its duties untrammeled. I bring to it a conscious desire and determination to fill it to the best of my ability to the satisfaction of the people."

THE BATTLE OF SEATTLE

- 1855 -

Two men, each one surrounded by his followers, looked at each other across the rough-hewn table. Several pieces of paper were spread out before them, and as each man spoke, an interpreter translated the words. The larger of the men was Seathl—a name now spelled *Seattle*—chief of the Duwamish and Suquamish Indians, two tribes of the Northwest Coast who made their homes in the region surrounding Puget Sound. The man opposite him was Isaac I. Stevens, governor of Washington Territory and the former U.S. Army topographical engineer who had helped survey a railroad route through Washington to the Pacific Ocean.

It was January 22, 1855, and Governor Stevens was on a self-appointed mission to negotiate for land with several Indian tribes in the region. Specifically, his meeting with Seathl was to clear the Puget Sound area of Indians so that white settlement could commence immediately. Before he was through with his tour in late 1855, Stevens had negotiated treaties with almost twenty tribes and acquired thousands of acres of virgin territory for white occupation.

Seathl signed such a treaty on that day in 1855, and as it turned out, that particular meeting was one of the easiest that Stevens had. The friendly old chief was eager to demonstrate his love and respect for the white man and recognized the inevitability of white domination in the area. The treaty stated that Seathl and his tribe were to be relocated to the Port Madison Reservation in today's Kitsap County.

Although Seathl was a leading advocate of establishing peace and tranquillity with the rapidly advancing white settlers, he still displayed great concern over the manner in which the newcomers treated the land. Shortly after the 1855 treaty signing with Governor Stevens, the patient chief expressed some of his misgivings.

> *There is no quiet place in the white man's cities. No place to hear the leaves of spring or the rustle of insect's wings. But perhaps because I am a savage and do not understand, the clatter only seems to insult the ears. And what is there to life if a man cannot hear the lovely cry of a whippoorwill or the arguments of the frogs around a pond at night? The Indian prefers the soft sound of the wind darting over the face of the pond, and the smell of the wind itself cleansed by a midday rain, or scented with a pinon pine. The air is so precious to the redman. For all things share the same breath—the beasts, the trees, the man. The white man does not seem to notice the air he breathes. Like a man dying for many days, he is numb to the stench. . . .*
>
> *What is man without the beasts? If all the beasts were gone, men would die from great loneliness of spirit, for whatever happens to the beast also happens to*

> *man. All things are connected. Whatever befalls the earth befalls the sons of the earth.*

White settlers had already begun to settle in Seathl's homeland before the treaty signing in 1855. As early as 1851 Americans had frequented Alki Point, across Elliott Bay from today's downtown Seattle. Later in the year more than a score of additional people landed and crowded themselves into two tiny log huts in the fog-enshrouded forest.

During 1852 most of the newcomers moved across the bay and established the village that became Seattle. Seathl, who by that time was already demonstrating his friendship with the white people, was cautious when the settlers proposed calling the new town "Seattle" in his honor. According to Katharine Judson in her book *Early Days in Old Oregon,*

> *He [Seathl] did not want his name used at first, because the Indians fear to have their name spoken after they are dead. Old Seattle was afraid his spirit would be troubled in the Ghost-Land, because he would hear it every time the name was spoken aloud. But the Americans made the kindly old chief so many presents that he was willing to take the risk. They told him, also that it was a very great honor.*

Unfortunately for both the Indians and the newly arrived settlers, Governor Stevens's peace initiative with the various Washington Indian peoples did not last. In late 1855 and 1856, several tribes took action against the settlers, and Stevens declared martial law. In January 1856 the infant village of Seattle, consisting of about twenty houses and a sawmill, was attacked by Indians. The settlers were supported by a small contingent of marines from the U.S. ship *Decatur.* After about a day of fighting, the settlers and marines, although badly outnumbered, prevailed, and the Indians, carrying with them their twenty-eight killed and eighty wounded, retreated. The Battle of Seattle was over.

Old Seathl maintained his friendship with the white pioneers all through the ordeal, never breaking his promise of peace. He died on the Fort Madison Reservation in 1866, at the age of nearly eighty.

INDIAN WARS

- 1858 -

Lieutenant Colonel William Jenner Steptoe, a forty-two-year-old graduate of West Point, marched from the stockade walls of Fort Walla Walla, Washington Territory, on May 6, 1858, with 164 men of the First Dragoons and the Ninth Infantry. Included in the column were a surgeon, a commissary officer, several civilian packers, a few friendly Nez Perce Indians, and two twelve-pound mountain howitzers. Their destination was the mining region around Colville, a small settlement almost two hundred miles north of the fort in the land between the Pend Oreille and Columbia Rivers.

Steptoe, an experienced officer from Virginia and a veteran of the Seminole and Mexican Wars, had been assigned to Washington Territory since 1854, shortly after being offered—and refusing—the governorship of Utah Territory. Almost from Steptoe's arrival, Washington Territory had been a hotbed of activity for several dissatisfied Indian groups, among them the Yakima, Spokane, Palous, and Coeur d'Alene tribes. Most of the Indians' unhappiness stemmed from the continuing encroachment upon tribal lands by white settlers and miners.

Territorial Governor Isaac I. Stevens, a former army officer and railroad surveyor, had set the stage for much of the unrest in the region. In May 1855 Stevens had negotiated treaties with about five thousand Indians of several tribes in the Walla Walla Valley. During a long and grueling meeting, the Indians had finally signed away most of their ancestral lands for a pittance. After promising the tribesmen that they could retain their homeland for several more years—until the treaty was ratified—less than two weeks later Stevens announced the opening of the Indian lands to white settlement.

In September 1856 the construction of Fort Walla Walla signified the army's intention to become a permanent presence in the region. By 1858 the influx of thousands of American miners and farmers into the eastern parts of Washington Territory had intensified the animosity the Indians felt toward whites. When Steptoe received a request from miners in the Colville region for protection against a suspected Indian uprising in the area, he responded by marching a column of soldiers north to negotiate with the Indians. This provided just the right heat for the pot to boil over.

On his way to Colville, Steptoe and his command were met by a contingent of several hundred Palous, Spokane, and Coeur d'Alene warriors who demanded that the soldiers leave natives' land and return to Fort Walla Walla. On May 17 Steptoe agreed to the Indians' request and turned his column south toward his command post. The Indians, in the meantime, had worked themselves into a frenzy, and even though Steptoe's command was working its way slowly southward, the Indians attacked the rear and sides of the column. Retreating to a knoll, Steptoe and his men fought off repeated assaults until dusk.

When Steptoe's command had left Fort Walla Walla earlier in the month, the colonel had cut the ammunition ration to each soldier to forty rounds, due to the extreme weight of the rest of the equipment and supplies that had to be carried on the backs of the pack animals. Now, after fighting all day, the men were down to three rounds each. Steptoe and his officers decided to leave the howitzers, camp supplies, and extra animals behind and to descend the butte under cover of darkness and rapidly retreat to safety.

Jack Dodd, the battle's historian, summarized the outcome of the battle in *Great Western Indian Fights.*

> *Two weeks had elapsed since the expedition had left. . . . In that time Steptoe's men had fought gallantly against a foe that outnumbered them eight to one, and had miraculously escaped from an almost certain massacre. The final losses were two officers, ten men, and three friendly Indians killed, plus ten men wounded, and 29 horses killed or lost from wounds in the "Battle of Tohoto-nim-me." The exact hostile losses are not known, but acknowledged losses were nine killed and 40 or 50 wounded.*

News of Steptoe's less than successful encounter with the Indians was met with disbelief among the authorities in the army's Department of the Pacific. Orders were immediately sent out to organize a new company, this time to be led by fifty-five-year-old Colonel George Wright, a longtime army regular and veteran of the Seminole and Mexican Wars, as well as of administrative duties as commander of the District of Columbia. Heading up several companies of the Ninth Infantry, the First Dragoons, and the Third Artillery, Wright left Fort Walla Walla on August 15, 1858, following several units of his command that had left previously to build a fort at the crossing of the Snake River. In all, close to seven hundred men and eight hundred animals accompanied Wright on his mission to exact retribution from the Indians who had sent Steptoe and his forces scurrying back to Fort Walla Walla.

Colonel Wright ordered his command to pitch camp at Four Lakes on the night of August 31, following a day that had been marked by increased Indian activity in the area. They were just a few miles southwest of today's bustling city of Spokane. By dawn of the next day, the Indians had occupied a nearby hill, and after a display of strength by the army, the Indians retreated down the north slope, taunting the soldiers all the way. Wright deployed various elements of his command, dislodging the Indians from their new post at the foot of the hill and sending the enemy into retreat. No U.S. Army soldiers were lost in this conflict known as the Battle of Four Lakes. About twenty Indians were killed and many more wounded.

Colonel Wright then marched northward and engaged the Indians again on September 5, in the Battle of Spokane Plains. As in the affair at Four Lakes, the army's sword-wielding dragoons, menacing artillery, and new, more accurate rifles used by the soldiers were too much for the Indian warriors, who were armed only with spears, bows and arrows, and inaccurate trade rifles.

After the wars of 1858 were over and the Indians realized that they were no match for the superior weaponry of the U.S. Army, peace, more or less, returned to Washington Territory. Each year that followed witnessed thousands of white emigrants flooding into the territory and taking permanent possession of what had been the Indians' ancestral lands.

LIEUTENANT MULLAN'S WAGON ROAD

- 1859 -

On January 24, 1861, in Olympia, Lyman Shaffer, the speaker of the House of Representatives of the nearly eight-year-old Washington Territory, wrote a letter to Lieutenant John Mullan of the U.S. Corps of Topographical Engineers. In the letter, Shaffer noted a resolution recently passed by the Washington territorial legislature thanking Mullan for his persistence in completing a wagon road. The resolution read:

> *Resolved by the Legislative Assembly of the Territory of Washington. That Lieut. John Mullan has the thanks of the Legislative Assembly of the Territory of Washington for his industry, energy, and ability in constructing the military road from Walla Walla to Fort Benton. And be it further Resolved that a copy of these resolutions duly certified shall be forwarded by the Secretary*

> *of the Territory to Lieut. John Mullan, the Secretary of War, the President of the United States, and our Delegate in Congress.*

John Mullan was a Virginian and a West Point graduate, class of 1852. He had assisted Governor Isaac Stevens in 1853 on his survey for a northern transcontinental railroad route to the Pacific Ocean. In March 1858 he had received orders from Washington, D.C., to proceed to The Dalles on the Columbia River to begin the preliminary work required to build a road through the northwestern wilderness from Fort Walla Walla in Washington Territory to Fort Benton, on the Missouri River in present-day Montana.

Fort Benton was rapidly gaining a reputation as a trading mecca on the upper Missouri. Completed in 1846 by Alexander Culbertson and originally named Fort Lewis, the fort underwent changes in 1850 and was rechristened Fort Benton. If a road could be built between Fort Benton, in its strategic position at the head of navigation on the mighty Missouri, and Fort Walla Walla, on a tributary of the Columbia, the potential for even farther-reaching trade networks was obvious. The construction did not materialize that year, however, and after fighting hostile Indians in the area during the fall, Mullan returned to Washington, D.C., for the winter.

On March 15, 1859, Lieutenant Mullan received orders from Captain A. A. Humphreys at topographical engineer headquarters to recommence work on the road. Humphreys also stated that an appropriation of $100,000 had been allotted for the work and gave Mullan some basic guidelines: "In conducting this operation, your attention will first be directed to making those parts of the route where the greatest difficulties and most numerous obstructions exist practicable for the passage of wagons at all seasons of the year."

Humphreys also ordered Mullan to figure the probable cost of building the road, to project the number of workers required and their salaries, and to estimate the overall expense of putting the work party in the field for sixteen months. After his plan and budget were approved by headquarters, Mullan received his final orders:

> *With your assistants and such employees as it may be found advisable to engage here, proceed to Fort Dalles, Oregon, via New York, where you will have collected and prepared as soon as practicable the tools, materials, and outfit requisite for the work, and employ mechanics, laborers, and other persons as may be necessary.*

By May 10 Lieutenant Mullan had arrived at The Dalles. During the next fifteen days, he hired the required workers, organized his force, and prepared for the rigorous, time-consuming work that lay ahead. Mullan had familiarized himself with the region during the days when he had assisted Governor Stevens on the railroad survey—and in fact had already determined the route the road would take. Although he knew the going would be rough, he probably didn't expect he would lose one of his men. In his official report, Mullan wrote of the incident.

> *I regret the loss of one of Lieutenant White's men by drowning while crossing the Snake River. He had been above the camp for wood, which he floated down the stream in the form of a raft; being upon which, the current, which is at the rate of five or six miles per hour, carried him so far below that, jumping off it, it was impossible to save him.*

Mullan and his men labored through the winter of 1859–60 amid extremely unfavorable conditions. Below-zero temperatures, the deaths of animals, below-standard provisions, difficult work cutting trees and building bridges—these were just a few of the obstacles that stood in the way of Mullan's mission. On August 1, 1860, however, the Mullan party finally reached Fort Benton, its objective completed.

Improvements to the road were made during 1861–62. When they were completed, the Mullan Road bridged the gap between the headwaters of two of the mightiest rivers of the West, the Missouri and the Columbia.

THE PIG WAR

- 1859 -

Brigadier General William Selby Harney could hardly believe his ears as he listened to the carefully phrased words one of his staff officers read to him. He had just dictated the letter to an aide, but the general was having difficulty realizing that the future of U.S.-claimed San Juan Island, in the strait that separated British-held Vancouver Island and mainland Washington, was in jeopardy because of a ludicrous act that had spiraled out of control.

It wasn't the first time Harney had been drawn into a potentially dangerous situation because of someone else's foolishness. Just four years earlier he had been summoned home from a European vacation to mount an expedition against the Sioux Indians. On that occasion a young, brash army lieutenant had opened fire on a Sioux encampment just outside Fort Laramie as he foolishly went to take prisoner a man who had shot a cow belonging to a Mormon emigrant.

This time, an international incident was about to erupt over the killing of a pig!

Dated August 7, 1859, Harney's letter to the adjutant general in Washington, D.C., summarized the situation.

> *A week or ten days before my arrival on that island [San Juan] one of the Americans shot a pig belonging to the Hudson's Bay Company, after having been greatly provoked by the person in charge, to whom he had applied to have the pig secured, as it damaged his fields. This request was treated with contempt, and the pig was shot, the American offering twice the value for the animal, which was refused.*

Harney, a product of the Tennessee frontier, had served in practically every conflict of the U.S. Army since he enlisted as a second lieutenant in the infantry in 1818. Now, after a career that had spanned more than forty years, he was the commander of the Department of Oregon, with military responsibilities over the entire northwestern United States. On a recent inspection tour of the posts under his command, Harney had visited the Americans who lived on San Juan Island. They told him of the dire situation that existed with the British authorities headquartered on Vancouver Island.

San Juan Island had been first permanently occupied in late 1853 by employees of the Hudson's Bay Company, who brought with them a herd of thirteen hundred sheep to graze the lush meadows of the island. The following year the legislative assembly of Washington Territory incorporated the island, along with parts of the mainland, into the newly formed county of Whatcom. When county officials attempted to collect taxes from the Hudson's Bay Company residents in 1855, they were rebuked. Accordingly, the sheriff seized and sold at auction thirty of the company's sheep. For the next few years,

Whatcom County officials continued to assess the British for their San Juan Island properties, but in order to keep the peace, they made no real effort to collect the revenues.

In the meantime San Juan Island had become the destination for several more Americans lured by the beauty and fertility of the place. The pig incident occurred during the summer of 1859. Charles McKay, an American resident of the island at the time of the incident, recorded his version of the event.

> *One day a hog belonging to the Hudson Bay Company broke into Cutler's potato patch. Cutler [Lyman Cutler, an American resident] went to the Company's agent and told him if he did not take care of this hog he would kill him [the hog]. The hog came and rooted all the potatoes. When Cutler came home the hog was still in his garden. He got his gun and shot the pig. Then he went to the Hudson Bay agent and offered to pay for the hog, but the agent refused to take pay and said he would send for the gunboat and have him arrested and taken to Victoria.*

In view of all the difficulties upon the island, its American residents requested that Harney send a detachment of men to protect them. Harney dispatched Captain George Pickett with sixty-eight men of the Ninth Infantry to secure the island. (Pickett would later become a Confederate general best remembered for his ill-fated charge at Gettysburg.) Within hours of Pickett's arrival, the British warship *Satellite* sailed into the harbor from Vancouver. When Pickett received a letter from the Hudson's Bay Company agent demanding his withdrawal, the thirty-four-year-old Virginian replied: "I do not acknowledge the right of the Hudson's Bay Company to dictate my course of action. I am here by virtue of an order from my government, and shall remain till recalled by the same authority."

Over the next few weeks, more British and U.S. forces were sent to the area. Several more British warships, bearing 167 guns and carrying more than two thousand men, were dispatched, only to be met by four hundred additional U.S. troops. Fortunately, after the excitement of the military movements was over, sense returned to both sides, and these two nations of common heritage and ancestry resolved their differences amicably. They eventually agreed to allow the German kaiser to act as mediator in determining the placement of the international border. In October 1872 it was decided that San Juan Island belonged to the United States.

THE NORTHWEST BOUNDARY SURVEY

- 1861 -

YOUNG ARMY OFFICER LIEUTENANT JOHN G. PARKE hacked his way through the dense temperate rain forest along the U.S.–Canada border. His mission was to assist in establishing the boundary line as defined by the British–U.S. Treaty of 1846, which recognized the forty-ninth parallel as the border between the two countries.

Parke had arrived in Washington in the spring of 1857 and established his base at Camp Simiahmoo, located on the Strait of Georgia near what is today the town of Blaine. From there, Parke intended to march overland through thick forests and across the high Cascade Mountains until he reached his final destination, the Continental Divide at the present-day junction of Montana, Alberta, and British Columbia. There, his survey line along the forty-ninth parallel would meet the treaty line of 1818, which extended from the western shore of Lake of the Woods west to the Continental Divide.

Lieutenant Parke was a seasoned engineer and surveyor. The thirty-year-old West Point graduate had assisted Lieutenant Lorenzo

Sitgreaves with his survey of the Zuni and Colorado Rivers in 1851 and was also involved in the government surveys for a trans-Mississippi railroad route to the Pacific Ocean. On this, his latest mission, he was assigned the duties of chief astronomer and surveyor.

Parke and his men left Camp Simiahmoo in June 1857. By the end of the 1858 work season, they had surveyed only ninety miles of the seemingly endless evergreen forests that stretched in all directions. They had entered the rugged Cascade Mountains, with peaks reaching upwards of nine thousand feet, and surveyed as far as the Skagit River valley.

During the last part of the 1858 season, a British survey party led by Colonel J. S. Hawkins of the Royal Engineers assisted Parke's crew. Although Great Britain and the United States had contended over San Juan Island, the men of the joint forty-ninth survey party got along admirably, since the 1846 treaty had really left no question about the inland border route. In his definitive history of the U.S. Corps of Topographical Engineers, *Army Exploration in the American West 1803–1863,* William H. Goetzmann writes, "Only once did the British and American parties disagree over the location of the line itself, and later conferences over the drafting table soon satisfied both parties."

As workers of the survey team laboriously marked the boundary line by cutting a path twenty feet wide through the dense forests, the surveyors and astronomers checked and double-checked their readings, entering the collected data on a map. They began the procedure again in spring 1859 and reached the Columbia River by the end of the working season.

By spring 1861 the joint American and British engineer party had completed its survey along the forty-ninth parallel, and the two groups disbanded and started for other assignments. Lieutenant Parke went to Washington, D.C., where he and the commissioner for the survey, Archibald Campbell, began the long and arduous task of assembling all the field data, maps, compass readings, natural history reports, artwork, and engineers' notes into a readable report.

Parke's work was interrupted later in the year when he accepted a captaincy in the engineer corps of the Union Army. In late November 1861 he was appointed brigadier general of volunteers. Eventually elevated to major general, he became General Ambrose Burnside's chief of staff and saw action at Antietam, Fredericksburg, Knoxville, and the Wilderness. After the Civil War Parke became the commandant at West Point and later moved to Washington, D.C., where he died in 1900.

Lieutenant Parke didn't know it when he was surveying the U.S.–Canada boundary line, but when he left the Washington wilderness in 1861, he was to be the last topographical engineer to see duty in the American West. The elite corps had been organized as part of the U.S. Army in 1838, and during its short but valuable service, its men had explored every corner of the plains and mountains of the trans-Mississippi region. According to Goetzmann, "The Topographical Engineers played the part of an advance guard as they collected and assembled an ever-mounting number of facts about a little-known area of the world. . . . Its officers were a new type of explorer, self-consciously carrying the burden of civilization to the wilderness and the lessons of the wilderness back into civilization."

Such noted explorers and engineers as Stephen Long, John C. Frémont, William H. Emory, and Joseph E. Johnston were all members of the Corps of Topographical Engineers at one time in their distinguished careers.

The Corps of Topographical Engineers ceased to be an independent army unit in 1863, at a time when many of its former members were fighting on one side or the other in the Civil War.

Although most of them served gallantly and are remembered for their Civil War services, as Goetzmann points out, "A far better memorial for these soldier-explorers lies in the rivers and the mountains of the Far West which they helped to discover and which still bear their names."

EXPLORATION OF THE OLYMPIC PENINSULA

- 1889 -

NEWS OF WASHINGTON'S ADMISSION INTO THE UNION was still only a few weeks old in late 1889 when Edmond S. Meany, a twenty-seven-year-old journalist for the *Seattle Press,* decided to form an expedition to explore the Olympic Peninsula. Meany's friends scoffed at the idea; after all, it was almost 1890. Washington had been settled for decades.

But Meany's friends didn't know that practically the entire Olympic Peninsula was still an untouched wilderness. Even today the peninsula maintains its wild character. In 1976 writer Richard L. Williams recorded his observations of the peninsula.

> *The Olympic Peninsula is an improbable physiographic assemblage of high-and-mighty mountain peaks, creeping glaciers, shadowy rain forests, brooding lakes, ferocious rivers and storm-battered shoreline. It remained*

> *pure wilderness for more than a century after the East Coast was tamed, and even now, in some of its fastnesses, it savages most human efforts to domesticate it.*

Adding to the mystery of the peninsula was the legend of the Thunder Bird, or *Thlew-cloots,* as the local Makah Indians called it. Thlew-cloots was a mysterious creature who dwelled in the remote mountains and rain forests of the region. Under its wings it carried a lightning snake, *Hah-hake-to-ak,* that assisted it in hunting. The story of the Thunder Bird was recorded from the local Indians by settler and Indian agent James G. Swan as early as the 1850s.

> *This Thunder Bird is an Indian of gigantic proportions, who lives on top of the mountains. His food is whales, and when hungry he puts on his wings and feathers as an Indian wraps himself in a blanket, and sails out in search of his prey. When a whale is discovered, the* Hah-hake-to-ak *darts out its fiery tongue, which kills the fish; and as the mighty bird settles down to seize it in its talons, the rustling of its great wings produces the thunder. The whale, when seized, is taken up into the mountain and devoured.*

Perhaps Meany was intrigued by the mysterious legend of the Thunder Bird, or motivated by the recent suggestion of the new governor, Elisha P. Ferry, that the time might be right for "unveiling the mystery which wraps the land encircled by the snow-capped Olympic range." Whatever his reasoning, Meany assembled six men to be sponsored by the *Seattle Press,* dubbed them the "Press

Exploring Expedition," and sent them on their way across Puget Sound to the Olympic Peninsula.

James H. Christie, a well-known Arctic explorer, led the group. Charles A. Barnes served as topographer. The party's equipment consisted of the usual wilderness camping gear, plenty of food, weapons and ammunition, four dogs, and fifty pounds of "colored fire," an explosive mixture to be set ablaze from the top of a high mountain on a particular night so that Meany, in Seattle, could monitor the group's progress.

The exploring party crossed Puget Sound in late December 1889. After landing at Port Angeles, the men spent several weeks building a flatboat with which to ascend the Elwha River, only to find out when the time came that the river was not navigable. After three months the explorers still had not reached the headwaters of the Elwha. Their food nearly exhausted, they survived by hunting deer and other wild game. Somewhere along the way the "colored fire" was jettisoned, since survival, not fireworks, was now foremost in the men's minds.

After weeks of wandering in the remote wilderness, climbing and misidentifying several mountain peaks along the way, the travelers ran into a white man and some Indians who carried the explorers in a canoe to the safety of Lake Quinault. From there Meany's expedition members made their way to the Pacific shore and thence down the coast to Aberdeen. Twenty-two weeks after they began their journey, the five men (one had left the mission earlier) of the Press Exploring Expedition became the first travelers on record to cross the Olympic Peninsula.

In July 1907 another group of Washingtonians took on the Olympic wilderness. Spurred on by the role model of President Theodore Roosevelt, the outdoorsmen, about seventy members of the Seattle Mountaineers Club, set out for the peninsula. By mid-August ten men and a woman had successfully climbed Mount Olympus, nearly eight thousand feet above the Pacific coast.

Today Olympic National Forest and Olympic National Park dominate the Olympic Peninsula. Forty-eight hours before he left presidential office in 1909, Theodore Roosevelt proclaimed six hundred thousand acres of the peninsular wilderness as the Mount Olympus National Monument. Three decades later President Franklin D. Roosevelt nearly doubled the size of the area and renamed it Olympic National Park. Since then U.S. Highway 101 has been extended to form a loop around the peninsula, making the region's savage beauty more accessible to all.

SEATTLE'S DEPARTURE-POINT CAMPAIGN

- 1897 -

For several days in early July 1897, residents of Seattle heard rumors of a fabulous gold strike in the Yukon Territory of Canada, several hundred miles north of the U.S.–Canada border. The precious metal had been discovered on a small tributary of the Klondike River during the summer of 1896. When news of the strike reached the United States, many would-be prospectors and miners headed north to try their luck in the diggings. By summer 1897 many of the newcomers had indeed struck it rich and were en route back to the United States to display their newfound wealth.

A July 15 extra edition of the *Seattle Daily Times* added to the widespread rumors.

FAIRY TALE OF THE FABULOUS WEALTH

Former Seattle Man Takes out $65,000!

MAY BE FACT OR FANCY

T. S. Lippy was the former secretary of the Seattle branch of the YMCA and one of many Seattle residents who had tried his luck in the Klondike. Upon his return he happily but cautiously told Seattle residents of his experience: "The place is rich. I hesitate to talk of this wealth, for it might induce people to go to the Klondike who are not fit to go. It is not an easy undertaking. It is filled with difficulties and trials one can hardly dream of."

But Lippy's admonition fell on deaf ears. His success in the Klondike gold fields, coupled with the arrival of the ship *Portland,* laden with successful prospectors and their gold, merely served to further excite the residents of Seattle. Hundreds of townspeople turned out to see the *Portland* pull into the slip at the Seattle dock; and many of them, then and there, decided to make the long trip north to get some of the riches for themselves.

As the weary but wealthy passengers disembarked, plans were also under way to make Seattle the jumping-off place for thousands of eager prospectors. Shrewd city officials determined to cash in on the Klondike gold rush whether they were personally involved in it or not. For them it was just as exciting, and much more profitable, to promote the town's strategic location as a departure point. As thousands upon thousands of gold-thirsting would-be miners passed through, Seattle would reap the benefits from the money they spent on supplies for the lengthy and hazardous journey to the Klondike.

In late August, as reported by a local newspaper, the Seattle Chamber of Commerce met to continue discussions for "widely advertising the city of Seattle as the principal outfitting point for Alaskan miners, and also to counteract the efforts of other cities in the same direction." Although Seattle was only forty-six years old with a population of only sixty-seven thousand, most of the chamber members felt that if an aggressive advertising campaign were launched, Seattle would be in a most desirable position to benefit from the Klondike fever.

The chamber hired Erastus Brainerd, a forty-two-year-old, unemployed Harvard graduate who had most recently been the Washington State land commissioner, to spearhead a project to put Seattle on the map once and for all. Within weeks Brainerd had masterminded a national advertising campaign extolling the benefits of the city as a departure point for those interested in going to the gold diggings. According to one ad, "Seattle has outfitted 90 percent of the persons who have gone to the Yukon, is doing so today, and can offer more satisfaction with less expense than can be done elsewhere."

Brainerd sent notices all over the United States and wrote several magazine articles about Seattle's ideal location. Inquiries came in so fast that a Bureau of Information was established within the Chamber of Commerce. Bureau employees replied to requests for information and continued the campaign of blitzing the country with promotional information about Seattle's outstanding position as the number one departure point for Klondike-bound travelers.

It didn't take long for Brainerd's publicity efforts to pay off. The thousands of emigrants who poured into the city by train from the East or by steamship around Cape Horn were met with information to help them get to the Klondike as rapidly and inexpensively as possible. Posted all over the city, broadsides directed the newcomers.

> *The City of Seattle has established a* BUREAU OF INFORMATION *for the purpose of giving visitors and strangers information as to Hotels, Lodging Houses, and Private Houses, also as to the Northern Mines, Transportation Lines, the Purchase of Supplies, and other matters in connection with the City and the Country to the North.*
>
> THIS INFORMATION IS FREE TO ALL. *To obtain it, call at the office at the corner of Columbia and Western Avenue, near the railroad.*

By September 1, 1897, nine thousand prospectors and their families had entered Seattle, outfitted themselves for the long trip north, and departed the city, most of them by steamship. Although the vast majority of them returned to the United States empty-handed, many did get lucky and strike it rich. By July 1898, when across most of the country a good Sunday meal cost a quarter and a hotel room could be had for fifty cents a night, the U.S. assay office in Seattle was processing nearly one million dollars' worth of gold every month. By that time, however, Seattle had already struck it rich from the thousands of dollars spent by the prospectors and miners just passing through.

A second gold rush in 1899, this one near Nome, Alaska, added to Seattle's economy as the city again assumed its role as primary departure point for northbound gold-seekers. Seattle attained such a favorable reputation as a progressive city that the Alaska-Yukon-Pacific Exposition held there in 1909 drew almost four million visitors from all over the world. When the 1910 census was completed, the city's population had grown to nearly a quarter of a million residents, many of them attracted there during the Klondike gold rush of 1897.

EDWARD CURTIS MEETS SUCCESS

- 1898 -

EDWARD S. CURTIS COULDN'T POSSIBLY HAVE KNOWN on a midsummer day in 1898 that his life would change forever. Curtis, a thirty-year-old photographer, was part owner of a photography studio in Seattle. Since his move to Washington from his native Wisconsin eleven years earlier, he had met with fair success in his photographic endeavors. His favorite subjects were the Indians who lived in the region around Puget Sound. Already some of his photographs of these striking people had won him several national awards.

Curtis was also an outdoorsman, a lover of nature, and an accomplished mountain climber. In fact, mountain climbing was the reason he was there on that day, plodding along the rock-strewn slopes of Mount Rainier, some fifty-five miles southeast of Seattle. Mount Rainier, an ice- and snow-clad volcanic peak jutting 14,410 feet above sea level, had been conquered only twenty-eight years earlier by two climbers who had almost died reaching their goal. Ever since, Mount Rainier had been eyed by cautious climbers as a formidable foe, a glacier-covered mass that experienced frigid temperatures even in the middle of summer.

Curtis had ascended partway up Mount Rainier to photograph the breathtaking scenery from the heights. Above the timberline, he could see for miles in all directions. It was those distant vistas that Curtis wanted to capture on his photographic plates.

While rambling along the treacherous slopes, his heavy camera and photographic equipment in tow, Curtis stumbled upon a party of climbers who, well equipped and seasoned looking as they were, were lost. The men were elated to see him. He quickly calmed their fears and assured them he knew the way down the mountain and would lead them to safety.

After the joy of being rescued had subsided, the men introduced themselves. It was only then that Curtis learned he was among three of the nation's leading conservation advocates and most eminent scientists. He shook frigid hands with Gifford Pinchot, chief of the U.S. Forestry Service; Dr. C. Hart Merriam, chief of the U.S. Biological Survey, forerunner of today's Fish and Wildlife Service; and George Bird Grinnell, editor of *Forest and Stream* magazine, renowned authority on the Cheyenne Indians, and founder of the Audubon Society.

The trio of eastern naturalists and Curtis became fast friends. The following year Curtis received an invitation to join the upcoming Harriman Expedition to Alaska as chief photographer. Named after its organizer and sponsor, railroad mogul Edward H. Harriman, the expedition had started out as a mere vacation for Harriman. But before he was through, the tycoon had converted his holiday into a full-blown, lavishly equipped scientific expedition that included fourteen members of his own family. Also included were twenty-five of America's foremost naturalists, artists, ethnographers, photographers, and geologists, as well as two of Curtis's new acquaintances, Merriam and Grinnell.

Returning to Seattle from Alaska in July 1899, Curtis busied himself with processing the several thousand photographs he and his assistant had taken. When the fourteen-volume Harriman Expedition report was published several years later by the Smithsonian Institution, Curtis's photographs embellished page after page.

Perhaps more important than the photographs was the germ of a grand idea that returned with Curtis to his studio. The notion would grow over the next several months. After visiting the Blackfeet Indian tribe with his friend Grinnell, Curtis finalized his thoughts and prepared to embark on an artistic journey that would take thirty years.

Curtis was convinced that he should photographically document the life and lifestyles of American Indians before they became more displaced and marginalized than they already were. With the enthusiasm of a zealot, Curtis embarked on his monumental project, hoping to pay for it out of the proceeds of print sales and income from his Seattle studio.

Curtis first visited the American Southwest. From there he traveled to the Great Plains and Rocky Mountains. In 1904 he returned to Seattle with more than one thousand negative plates depicting life among the various Pueblo tribes, the Apaches, the Navajos, and the many agricultural tribes that lived along the Colorado River, as well as the Sioux, Cheyenne, Blackfeet, Nez Perce, Crow, and other plains and mountain tribes.

A successful exhibit of his photographs in Seattle earned him an invitation to come to Washington, D.C., and display his work there. While in the capital Curtis was introduced to President Theodore Roosevelt, who showed great interest in his project. Several magazine articles illustrated with his photographs and a lecture tour in the East enhanced Curtis's growing reputation. Roosevelt arranged an appointment for Curtis to meet with the financier J. P. Morgan, and when the two men parted, Curtis had Morgan's assurance of financial backing for the publication of his photographs in book form, "the handsomest ever published."

For the next twenty-one years, Curtis traveled the length and breadth of the American West photographing Indians of many tribes, both on and off reservations. Eighty tribes were represented in more than forty thousand photographs. The first volume of Curtis's opus was published in 1907. It carried a title page that accurately described the effort.

> The North American Indian
>
> *Being a series of Volumes Picturing and Describing the Indians of the United States and Alaska, written, illustrated and published by Edward S. Curtis, edited by Frederick Webb Hodge, foreword by Theodore Roosevelt, field research conducted under the patronage of J. Pierpont Morgan, in twenty volumes.*

Twenty-three years later, the twentieth and final volume of *The North American Indian* rolled off the presses. The complete set of volumes was produced in a limited edition of five hundred copies. Although fewer than two hundred complete sets of the work had been sold by 1930, the complete set immediately became a collector's item.

Curtis eventually left Seattle and, while continuing his photographic interests, became involved in several mining enterprises. He died in Los Angeles in 1952, never realizing that someday a complete set of twenty volumes of text and twenty portfolios of photographs of *The North American Indian*—when it could be found—would command a price of several hundred thousand dollars, a far cry from the three thousand dollar issue price.

THE CREATION OF MOUNT RAINIER NATIONAL PARK

- 1899 -

THE TWO MEN QUICKLY AND QUIETLY congratulated each other as they braced themselves against the miserably cold wind and below-zero temperatures. They had just reached the summit of Washington's Mount Rainier and were the first documented climbers to conquer the seventh-highest peak in the United States. As they stood in the rapidly approaching dusk amid falling temperatures, their accomplishment must have been the least of their considerations. At almost 14,500 feet above sea level, they had to find shelter in a hurry. They realized it would be impossible to descend the slopes before nightfall.

The year was 1870, and the two climbers, P. B. Van Trump and Hazard Stevens, were both hardy outdoorsmen and experienced woodsmen. But never before in their lives had they witnessed a place like the summit of Mount Rainier. Luckily the summit crater was riddled with ice caves hollowed out by steam escaping from the many volcanic vents around the rim of the crater. The two found a degree of shelter in one of the caves and, miraculously, survived until the next morning, when they thankfully began their descent.

Mount Rainier is a natural wonder of opposite extremes. Although outside temperatures near the summit can reach -80 degrees Fahrenheit, the temperature of the steam generated from the volcanic vents sometimes climbs to 170 degrees, a difference of 250 degrees.

The first documented sighting of the mountain was in the late 1700s. Captain George Vancouver, the British seaman who sailed along the Washington and Oregon coasts, named it Mount Rainier in honor of another British naval officer. The peak, perched amid the mighty Cascade Mountains and visible for miles around Puget Sound, was called "Tacoma" by many of the Indians in the vicinity.

By the 1890s there was a great deal of local interest in preserving the rapidly deteriorating wilderness around Mount Rainier. Already, timber companies, awed by the tremendous abundance of quality pine, cedar, and fir forests in the Pacific Northwest, had constructed roads into many areas. Cyrus A. Mosier, an agent of the U.S. Department of the Interior, was sent west in 1891 to study the prospect of government creation of forest reserves, the forerunner of today's national forests. Mosier was shocked by conditions in the region—conditions perpetrated not only by the timber companies, but by careless and unconcerned campers as well. He recommended that the government take immediate steps to preserve what was left of these pristine forests. Two years later, in 1893, President Benjamin Harrison signed legislation establishing the Pacific Forest Reserve, a vast region of Washington wilderness including today's Mount Rainier National Park.

When the Pacific Forest Reserve was established, the nation had four national parks—Yellowstone, Yosemite, Sequoia, and General Grant. Upon the creation of the forest reserve, efforts got under way to make Mount Rainier and its surrounding wilderness into a fifth national park. The move was instigated by Washington's Senator Watson C. Squire, who presented a petition from the Seattle Chamber of Commerce to the U.S. Congress. The General Land Office was opposed to the idea, and its commissioner persuaded the secretary of the interior to soft-pedal it was well. But by 1896, when several leading easterners got behind the movement, the tide slowly began to turn in favor of establishing a national park in Washington State.

Then another obstacle presented itself. In 1864, when the Northern Pacific Railroad promised to push its rail line all the way to the Pacific Ocean, one of the concessions it received from the federal government was the title to several thousand square miles of the territory through which the rail line would run. Before a national park could be created for the Mount Rainier region, the government had to reacquire all of that railroad land in exchange for federal lands elsewhere. By the time these real estate dealings were complete, three more years had passed.

Finally, however, on March 2, 1899, President William McKinley signed the bill establishing Mount Rainier National Park. Although the residents of Washington were jubilant that the park had finally been set aside, they were not happy with its name. During the long negotiations for the park's creation, the name associated with the proposed project had been Washington National Park. There was also widespread interest, especially among residents of Tacoma, in naming it Mount Tacoma National Park and to change the name of Mount Rainier to Mount Tacoma. In the end, last-minute congressional maneuvering resulted in the name change to Mount Rainier National Park, as it is still called today. Encompassing nearly a quarter of a million acres, the park has accommodated millions of visitors since its creation in 1899.

MR. WEYERHAEUSER'S SURPRISE

- 1900 -

ON NOVEMBER 17, 1899, FREDERICK WEYERHAEUSER, a onetime penniless German immigrant, arrived at the train station in Tacoma, Washington. As he stepped from his private car, surrounded by his son, his partner, a lawyer, a banker, and several timber associates, he was swamped by a large crowd. As usual, Weyerhaeuser attracted a swarm of newspapermen and photographers. For now, the sixty-five-year-old patriarch was poor no more. From his humble beginnings in America in 1852, when he made thirteen dollars a month as a farm laborer, Weyerhaeuser had risen to become the nation's richest and most influential timber man, and his fame had spread all over the world.

Since timber was already big business in Washington, practically everyone at the train station recognized this modestly dressed gentleman from back east. What piqued the curiosity of most of the spectators was why he was here in the Pacific Northwest, hundreds of miles from his base of operations in Minnesota. An aggressive journalist for the *Tacoma Evening News,* unable to bear the suspense any longer, popped the obvious question. Weyerhaeuser ignited the crowd's enthusiasm when he replied, "You have plenty of fine timber in Washington, and so has your southern neighbor, Oregon. We are just looking around on this trip. We may buy a great deal of timberland here and we may start up several mills. We'll see what can be done."

It shouldn't have struck Washingtonians as strange that a timber magnate like Weyerhaeuser would eventually express interest in the thousands of square miles of virgin timber that clothed the Cascade Mountains. After all, a railroad now connected Duluth, Minnesota, and Portland, Oregon, and another linked Minneapolis, Minnesota, and Seattle, Washington. Both lines were capable of providing fast and inexpensive transportation of lumber to users in the Mississippi Valley and points farther east. The restriction that had once severely limited the movement of large shipments of timber eastward across the Great Plains had finally been overcome. The Pacific Northwest was ripe for massive expansion of its timber operations, and Weyerhaeuser was just the man who could provide the leadership and the resources to accomplish this growth.

Another circumstance favoring Weyerhaeuser was that his friend and business associate James J. Hill had recently gained control of the Northern Pacific Railroad, adding it to his own Great Northern Railway. In acquiring the Northern Pacific, Hill had also inherited forty-four million acres of prime northwestern land granted to the Northern Pacific by the U.S. government as right-of-way. Hill had no use for the land and offered it for sale to Weyerhaeuser.

It didn't take Weyerhaeuser long after his return to St. Paul, Minnesota, to make his plans known. On January 3, 1900, his office announced that the Weyerhaeuser Group intended to purchase a total of nine hundred thousand acres of prime Douglas-fir forestland, most of it in Washington, from the Northern Pacific Railroad. The purchase price was six dollars an acre, or about ten cents per thousand board feet! Weyerhaeuser's surprise purchase was one of the largest real estate transactions in U.S. history.

Frederick Weyerhaeuser's entrance into the Pacific Northwest theater of timber operations was the beginning of a long-range relationship between his company and the land, forests, and people of Washington, Oregon, and Idaho. To this day the corporate colossus maintains a strong presence throughout the area, and many thousands of the region's residents rely on the company for their livelihoods.

Washington's timber industry grew and grew. By 1905 loggers were cutting nearly four billion board feet of wood per year, placing the state in the number one position in the United States for timber production, a spot it held until 1938. Today timber remains one of Washington's top natural resources.

THE CAPTURE OF HARRY TRACY

- 1902 -

RUMORS WERE AS THICK THAT AUGUST AS ripening wheat in the golden fields outside Creston, Washington. The town marshal, Charles Straub, had heard most of the tales and dismissed them one by one as the figment of someone's creative imagination. But when he received an eyewitness account of the notorious killer and prison escapee Harry Tracy's presence on a nearby farm, he decided that this was one long shot that he needed to investigate personally.

Marshal Straub entered George Dodd's barbershop, just down the street from his office, where he found four local men waiting to get their hair cut. Straub discussed with them the tip he had just received about Tracy's possible whereabouts. The men—Oscar Lillengreen, Maurice Smith, Joe Morrison, and Dr. E. C. Lander—agreed to help the marshal find Tracy. Straub quickly deputized the men and told them to meet at his office, where he would provide weapons and have transportation to the farm ready. A few minutes after the new deputies had armed themselves, the five lawmen climbed into a hired rig and started for the farm, where they hoped to find and capture the notorious outlaw.

The eminent western historian James D. Horan has called Tracy "the Tiger of the Wild Bunch . . . a fast drawing killer, a fighting machine without a bit of human dignity." Tracy, a native of New York, had joined Butch Cassidy's notorious Wild Bunch at the gang's hideout in the Hole-in-the-Wall country of Wyoming in 1896 when he was about twenty-seven years old. Already a fugitive on a murder warrant from Utah, Tracy didn't take long to fit right in with the gang's members, among them Cassidy, Harry Longabaugh ("the Sundance Kid"), Harvey Logan ("Kid Curry"), and George Curry.

Back then, the law had finally caught up with Tracy, and he was sent to prison in Aspen, Colorado. But he escaped soon afterward and made his way to Oregon, where again he was arrested and sentenced to prison, this time in Salem, Oregon. A little over three years later, in June 1902, Tracy escaped the Salem prison, killing several guards in the process, and headed north to Washington. The murder of the prison guards and Tracy's bad reputation put every law enforcement officer in the Pacific Northwest on the alert as one of the nation's largest manhunts began.

Just a few miles into their new-won freedom, Tracy and his most recent accomplice, Dave Merrill, were surrounded by a fifty-man posse near Gervais, Oregon. Miraculously, they escaped. By the time the pair reached Portland, the governor had called out 250 militiamen to join in the massive manhunt. But once again Tracy managed to evade his pursuers by forcing a local boatman to take him and Merrill across the Columbia River to Washington. Crossing the state border into Washington did not mean safety for the two outlaws. As the pair fled north toward Tacoma, both the reward money for their capture and the size of the posse increased. The governor of Washington gave orders to shoot to kill.

Soon after arriving in Tacoma, Tracy killed his partner when he learned that Merrill had sold him out to authorities years earlier in exchange for a lighter prison sentence. Alone, Tracy commandeered a fishing craft on Puget Sound and forced its captain to carry him to Seattle. There, at a farmhouse, the elusive killer was once again almost captured, only to shoot several men and make his escape.

On the run again, Tracy turned east and made his way toward Spokane. In Lincoln County, near the little community of Creston, he had decided to hole up for a while and let the news of his escape and killing spree die down. But his reputation was about to catch up with him for the last time.

When Marshal Straub's little posse reached the farm that August day, they found three men working on a barn. Tracy's photograph had been all over the front pages of the local newspapers lately, and as Straub and his men neared the three workers, Straub noticed that one of them bore a striking resemblance to the pictures. Straub quickly identified himself as a law officer and called out for Tracy to surrender. Instead of obeying orders, the outlaw grabbed his nearby rifle, fired a few shots, and disappeared into the billowing wheat fields that surrounded the farm.

Darkness soon arrived, and the five lawmen took up positions around the border of the wheat field. They knew Tracy was a vicious killer, so they wisely decided to wait until daylight to go in after him. Sometime during the wee hours of the night, the posse heard a single shot. As soon as dawn broke, Straub and his men carefully closed in. But there was to be no shootout, for they found Tracy dead. They noticed that he had been wounded in the leg and had bled badly during the night. It seemed the outlaw had killed himself rather than bleed to death or run the risk of going back to prison. Tired of running, Harry Tracy had finally put an end to it all on August 5, 1902, in that wheat field near Creston, Washington.

THE GREAT YACOLT FIRE

- 1902 -

SEPTEMBER 12, 1902, DAWNED A SULTRY DAY in the great Douglas-fir forests that dominated the vast territory between the Cascade Mountains and the Pacific Ocean, from northern California to the far reaches of British Columbia. Although smoke hung low over the thick forest along the Lewis River of southern Washington, no one thought a great deal about it, since small fires in the woods were common occurrences back then.

Around noon, Mr. and Mrs. Ira Reid, Mr. and Mrs. C. A. McKeen, six children, and George Smith, a visiting uncle from Kansas, set out in a horse-drawn wagon from the Reid farm on the north fork of Lewis River. They were going on a picnic to beautiful Trout Lake, nestled on the slope of Mount St. Helens, several miles to the north. They passed the tiny town of Vale and traveled along the logging road for another two miles or so before running into a solid sheet of fire that had swept down a nearby mountain valley.

Several weeks later, when Charlie Hartsuck and Charlie Smith rummaged their way through the thousands of burned Douglas-fir spires looking for survivors, they came upon the Reid wagon and the charred bodies of the fire's victims. The men saw the remains of the wagon first. Nothing was left but the iron wheels and hardware that had collapsed with the wagon when it burned. Then, within 150 feet of the wagon, the two men found the bodies of all eleven people. The remains of the two horses, released from the wagon by a frantic but kind master, were located a few feet beyond those of the humans. Speelyai Creek—which would have meant probable safety for the people and animals—was only one hundred yards away from the site of the tragedy.

At about the same time that the eleven had meet their doom, most of the residents on the nearby Newton farm had made it to the safety of Speelyai Creek when they saw the flames rapidly descending on them. Mrs. Newton, who stayed behind to rescue her Singer sewing machine and some jarred fruit, never made it to the creek.

The mailman who served these outlying farms was W. E. Newhouse. He had seen the fire approaching his house, hitched his horses to his mail buggy, and made a run for it. Several days later, both Newhouse and his horses were found, burned almost beyond recognition.

In the same neighborhood, Joe Polly had been awakened by cinders from the rapidly approaching firestorm falling on his roof. He made a run for it and luckily lived to tell the story. Polly's sister-in-law, a few miles away, was killed when the flames engulfed her, her baby, and her younger brother.

Although the big fires of 1902 are collectively referred to as the Yacolt blaze, the inferno's flames never reached the town of Yacolt. The fire came so close, however, that it blistered the paint on the town's frame buildings and sent nearly all the residents fleeing to the safety of a nearby creek.

Several other people and many animals had been killed throughout Clark County in the 1902 fires. A few days after the tragedy, a correspondent for Vancouver's weekly newspaper, the *Columbian,* reported, "What a week ago was a beautiful valley of the Lewis River is now a hot and silent valley of death, spotted with the blackened bodies of both man and beast."

Other regional newspapers reported the progress of the inferno as well. From Bucoda, Washington: "This town was inky darkness until noon today, and people were going around with lanterns. No fire is in sight as this is written but there must be great conflagrations somewhere else in the vicinity."

The Elma, Washington, newspaper proclaimed:

> *A courier has just arrived from the Star sawmill which he says has been wiped out. Men there made a brave fight but had to flee for their lives. The fire can be heard here in the village and it is like the sound of the sea as it crosses the bar. Ashes are falling like the skirmish before a snow storm. Wagonloads of refugees and their household effects are arriving in town.*

Stories of the fires' origins varied depending upon which newspaper one read. The Vancouver, Washington, paper erroneously reported that, "It is believed by many people that the big fires raging in this part of the state are due to an eruption from a volcanic source somewhere between Mount Hood and Mount St. Helens." Even from as far away as Eugene, Oregon, the damage could be felt and seen. The newspaper there proclaimed that, "The smoke is so heavy here that Skinners Butte cannot be seen from 8th street, four blocks away."

When it was all over, the fires had destroyed hundreds of farms, ranches, and sawmills. Cinders covered Portland, Oregon, to a depth of one-half inch. The fires stretched from Bellingham, Washington, to Eugene, Oregon, eventually burning more than seven hundred thousand acres of prime, virgin-growth Douglas fir, Sitka spruce, hemlock, and cedar. Whether the monstrous fires, numbering more than one hundred in all, were caused by human or natural acts will probably never be known.

The fires of 1902 caused an estimated $13 million worth of property damage alone, not counting the loss of human life and the billions of board feet of prime timber. Three years after the fires had damaged much of western Washington and Oregon, the state of Washington enacted a law that established a board of forest commissioners empowered to appoint a state fire warden and a number of deputies. Thus, Washington laid plans to reduce the possibility of a similar fire season from ever occurring again.

WILLIAM BOEING'S VISION

- 1916 -

William E. Boeing was inspired when he arrived home in Seattle in January 1910. The twenty-eight-year-old timber man had just been to Los Angeles to witness the first-ever U.S. air meet and had watched in awe as local pilots and French aviators matched their wits and flying machines. All the way back to Seattle, Boeing thought about what he had seen in California. He knew in his heart that aviation was poised on the edge of a new frontier and that whoever took advantage of the situation was sure to be successful.

Many of Boeing's countrymen did not share his enthusiasm. Even the prestigious *Scientific American* magazine scoffed at the idea of mankind participating in large-scale flying when it told its readers that same year, "To affirm that the airplane is going to revolutionize the future is to be guilty of the wildest exaggeration." But Boeing was a visionary and a dreamer, and he knew from the moment he had watched American and French pilots trying to outmaneuver each other in the southern California skies that he would spend his life perfecting the airplane.

Boeing realized that it was normal for Americans to look cautiously toward a future with flying as a means of transportation. After all, it had been only a little over six years since the brothers Orville and Wilbur Wright had gained worldwide prominence by successfully flying their homemade airplane at Kitty Hawk, North Carolina. Wilbur Wright had underscored the importance of the moment: "These flights were the first in the history of the world in which a machine carrying a man had raised itself into the air by its own power in free flight, had sailed forward on a level course without reduction of speed and had finally landed without being wrecked."

For five years Boeing could do little to fulfill his dream of becoming a major aircraft manufacturer. In 1915, however, he learned to fly, and a year later he built his first airplane based on a design by U.S. naval officer Conrad Westervelt. It was a small, twin-engine seaplane consisting of a linen-covered wooden frame held together with wire. The plane was appropriately called B&W, after Boeing and Westervelt.

The same year the B&W was introduced, Boeing incorporated his company and called it the Pacific Aero Products Company. Two years later the name was changed to Boeing Airplane Company.

Young Boeing knew he was on shaky ground in the fledgling industry of building airplanes when he described the company's mission to its few employees: "We are embarked as pioneers upon a new science and industry in which our problems are so new and unusual that it behooves no one to dismiss any novel idea . . . our job is to keep everlastingly at research and development."

During World War I, the Boeing Airplane Company provided planes for the U.S. Navy. But like many other manufacturers across the country, Boeing's company fell on hard times when government contracts dried up at the end of the war. In order to continue his profitable business, Boeing conceived of the idea of airplane-transported mail. In 1919 he and fellow pilot Eddie Hubbard flew to Vancouver, British Columbia, picked up the mail, and returned to Seattle, thus becoming the first purveyors of international air mail in history.

For the next few years the Boeing Airplane Company designed and manufactured several types of aircraft. By the time Charles Lindbergh awed the world with his successful nonstop flight across the Atlantic Ocean in 1927, Boeing had eight hundred employees and was a leader among aircraft companies in the United States. A year later the company introduced the nation's first airplane designed for civilian transportation and added the model to its fleet of planes in a subsidiary company, Boeing Air Transport, the predecessor of today's United Airlines. Originally designed to carry twelve passengers, the plane model was later enlarged to carry eighteen passengers, and the first stewardesses were hired at $125 per month.

William Boeing retired in 1934 and went on to pursue other interests. Meanwhile, the company he founded was busy with a new airplane, the world-famous B-17 "Flying Fortress." This mainstay of the U.S. Army Air Forces during World War II was first flown in prototype form in 1935. In January of the following year, the army ordered thirteen of the models. A contemporary description of the plane, which one authority has called "perhaps the most celebrated aircraft operated by the United States during the war," reads as follows:

> *This four-engine giant weighs 47,500 pounds, has a top speed of 300 m.p.h. and a range of 3,500 miles. It carries a bomb load of 10,000 pounds which is double that of most German, Italian and British bombers. Power-driven gun turrets are located in the nose, tail, and midship. Quarter-inch armor plate protects all*

crew positions except that of the tail gunner. Self-sealing bulletproof gasoline tanks are installed.

Following on the heels of the B-17 were the equally successful B-29 and B-52 bombers. In January 1957 three B-52s circumnavigated the globe nonstop in forty-six hours, a far cry from the ancient B&W first produced by Boeing forty-one years earlier. During the late 1950s and the 1960s, the Boeing Airplane Company turned its attentions to domestic travel and designed a whole new series of luxury jetliners, including the 707, 727, 737, and 747 models. In 1990 a variant of the 747 was converted into "Air Force One" and became the official plane of the president of the United States.

After his retirement in 1934, William Boeing devoted himself to personal pursuits. He was an accomplished horseman, pleasure sailor, and deep-sea fisherman. He donated his former home in Seattle to the Orthopedic Hospital and moved to his farm in Fall City. The man who had been awarded a Guggenheim Medal for "successful pioneering in aircraft manufacturing and air transport" died on September 28, 1956, on board his yacht *Taconite* while cruising in Puget Sound.

THE SEATTLE GENERAL STRIKE

- 1919 -

ON FEBRUARY 6, 1919, WHEN THE 10 A.M. SHIFT WHISTLE BLEW at the city's many shipyards, the people of Seattle witnessed a frightening silence. The usual hustle and bustle of hundreds of carriages, wagons, and automobiles had disappeared from the downtown streets. Even the main thoroughfares were devoid of traffic. All was deathly silent, and to a visitor Seattle must have seemed like a ghost town. Mayor Ole Hanson later described the scene: "Streetcar gongs ceased their clamor; newsboys cast their unsold papers into the street; from the doors of mill and factory, store and workshop, streamed sixty-five thousand workingmen. School children with fear in their hearts hurried homeward. The life stream of a great city stopped."

Five days later, on February 11, most affairs returned to normal in Seattle. The streets once again filled with pedestrian and vehicular traffic, schools reopened, and factories and mills, on the surface at least, operated as if nothing had ever happened. But the people of Seattle knew that, indeed, something momentous had just occurred.

They had just witnessed, for almost a week, the first general labor strike in U.S. history.

The Seattle General Strike of 1919 was a symptom of economic turmoil in America and most of Europe as well. Seething unrest was commonplace at the time in both the United States and among its former allies—and enemies. Just fifteen months earlier, the Russian Revolution had presented an entirely new approach to worker-government relations, and the severe war reparations placed upon vanquished German factory owners and workers alike by the Allies had left Germany a hotbed for revolution. Labor movements, both here and abroad, were coming into their own and were often led by strong personalities who were adept at channeling the discontent among workers.

The Industrial Workers of the World (IWW), whose members were called "Wobblies," was formed in 1905. The new organization's constitution read in part:

> *The working class and the employing class have nothing in common. There can be no peace so long as hunger and want are found among millions of working people and the few, who make up the employing class, have all the good things of life.*
>
> *Between these two classes a struggle must go on until the workers of the world organize as a class, take possession of the earth and the machinery of production, and abolish the wage system. . . .*
>
> *Instead of the conservative motto, "A fair day's wage for a fair day's work," we must inscribe on our banner the revolutionary watchword, "Abolition of the wage system."*

The Seattle strike of 1919 was sparked by organizers within the American Federation of Labor (AFL). It also had the strong support of the Wobblies and their followers. The local AFL movement shared much of the IWW's philosophy, and one of its spokesmen wrote, "I believe that 95 percent of us agree that the workers should control the industries." With the majority of Seattle's labor unions and workers subscribing to this position, the AFL planned its massive strike against Seattle shipbuilders, a strike that was soon embraced by practically all the city's industrial workers.

One of the local newspapers, the *Star,* ran an editorial that pleaded with workers to refrain from such drastic action.

> *This is plain talk to the common-sense union men of Seattle.*
>
> *You are being rushed pell-mell into a general strike. You are being urged to use a dangerous weapon—the general strike, which you have never used before—which, in fact, has never been used anywhere in the United States.*
>
> *It isn't too late to avert the tragic results that are sure to come from its use.*

Neither newspaper editorials nor pleas from civic leaders had any effect on the strike organizers. On the morning of February 6, 1919, as ordered, more than sixty thousand AFL workers stayed away from their jobs at the shipyards. Forty thousand other working people also failed to report to their jobs, either because they were afraid or, in many cases, because they simply couldn't get to work because of the citywide shutdown. Seattle had come to a standstill.

By 1:30 the first afternoon, the U.S. Army was placed on standby alert in the event it was needed for crowd control. The Seattle Police Department added six hundred new members. On the following day, the *Star*'s front page carried a statement by Mayor Hanson in which he promised "absolute and complete protection" to all citizens.

The general strike dragged on for five and a half days. Finally, by noon on Tuesday, February 11, the general strike was called off, and all the sympathy strikers went back to their jobs, although the shipyard workers remained on strike. Mayor Hanson's strong, hardheaded response had broken the general strike. His threat of government takeover of the striking facilities caused many workers to have second thoughts about their actions. Nonetheless, the shipyard workers remained on strike throughout the summer and into the following winter. By then, many of the large shipbuilders, unable to produce, had lost contracts, and thousands of striking workers were laid off.

The nation's first general strike was a dismal failure. Historian Robert L. Friedheim wrote that the strike was doomed before it began. "The Seattle general strike is a textbook example of the ineffectiveness of the non-revolutionary general strike as a labor weapon for attaining anything but the narrowest goals." In the end it seems all the people of Seattle suffered.

A WASHINGTON CONSERVATIONIST GOES TO COURT

- 1939 -

ORVILLE DOUGLAS HAD LOVED THE OUTDOORS for as long as he could remember. The young boy who would later become famous as U.S. Supreme Court Justice William O. Douglas roamed the Cascade Mountains of Washington as a youngster. He became so ingrained with the ways of the wilderness that his interest in wildlife, conservation, and the environment followed him for the rest of his life. By the time he was a teenager, Douglas was an experienced hiker, camper, and observer of nature, activities he pursued throughout much of his adopted state of Washington.

Born in Minnesota in 1898, Douglas spent a few years in California as a young child, then moved with his family to Yakima, Washington, when his father, a Presbyterian minister, was offered a position in the ministry there. Douglas attended Yakima High School and played on the basketball team. Whether he was playing high school sports or hiking in the rugged forests of the high Cascade Mountains, his physical prowess was all the more remarkable because he had suffered a severe bout of polio as an infant, which had left his legs in a weakened condition.

Douglas prevailed in his studies as well as in his physical endeavors. Upon graduation from high school, he enrolled in Whitman College in Walla Walla, Washington, on scholarship. He returned to Whitman after a short stint in the army during World War I and graduated in 1920 at the age of twenty-one.

After a couple of years of teaching at Yakima High School, Douglas was accepted to Columbia Law School in New York. In order to finance the transcontinental trip, he hired on with a local outfit to assist in the rail transport of two thousand sheep from Washington to Chicago. Riding in the caboose, he kept a watchful eye on his charges in the forward livestock cars. After many days of trials and tribulations for the weary Douglas, the train finally arrived in Chicago, and he disposed of the sheep. Days later Douglas pulled in to New York City with only six cents in his pocket. The following day he registered for law school.

Douglas completed Columbia Law School with little difficulty and took a job with a Wall Street law firm. He later joined the faculty of Yale University Law School, where the dean called him "the nation's outstanding teacher of law." For three years Douglas acted as a Securities and Exchange Commission (SEC) investigator and looked into brokerage firms and their roles in the 1929 stock market crash. It was no surprise in 1937 when Douglas was appointed chairman of the SEC. And there he served until his U.S. Supreme Court days began two years later.

When Justice Louis Brandeis announced his retirement from the high court in 1939, President Franklin Roosevelt began an immediate search for his replacement. Roosevelt looked for a westerner to fill the vacant position. *Time* magazine reported on the prospective appointment in February 1939.

> *Several names, none of them a standout, were in the air. Then something happened: a journalist friend recollected that extremely able Chairman William Orville Douglas of the SEC, 40, was born in Minnesota, lived in the state of Washington from 1904 to 1922, hence is a Westerner. . . . Mr. Douglas was called to the White House. When the President left town without making any appointments, the Douglas trial-balloon was still in the air.*

Douglas's name stayed in the front of the news, however. The following month, *Time* again reported on the Supreme Court vacancy. By this time, the new appointment had been made.

> *This week, the President named Mr. Douglas to be the youngest Associate Justice since Joseph Story, who was but 32 when President Madison appointed him in 1811 for a term that lasted 34 years. . . . A lot of Washington's younger, less social folk, and proprietors of various quick-order restaurants, were thrilled to the core at the prospect of already knowing a real, live, Scotch-drinking, story-telling member of the Supreme Court. . . . Besides work he [Douglas] likes golf, bridge, wild life, and sunsets.*

Douglas sat on the bench of the U.S. Supreme Court for nearly thirty-seven years, serving under five chief justices and seven presidents, "a record that may never be equaled," according to Chief Justice Warren Burger. When he retired in 1975, Douglas had served on the court longer than any other justice in U.S. history. A stroke earlier in the year had left him crippled and, as he described it, "bothered with incessant and demanding pain, which depleted my energy to the extent that I have been unable to bear my full share of the burden."

Despite the tremendous workloads placed upon Douglas during his long judicial career, his childhood love of wildlife and interest in preserving the environment never left him. He found time to travel the world extensively, usually visiting out-of-the-way places, and wrote a total of twenty-six books, many of them about the beauty and variety of nature. In one of them, *My Wilderness: The Pacific West,* published in 1960, he shared his wilderness philosophy with his readers. Completing the chapter about Mount Adams, a peak in south-central Washington especially dear to his heart, Douglas wrote:

> *I realized from my day's journey how badly we need high alpine meadows which can only be reached on foot, how badly we need peaks which can only be conquered by daring. The passion to bring "civilization" into our wilderness areas is one sign that we Americans are getting soft and flabby. We want everything made easy. Yet success is worth having only when it comes through great effort and hazardous exertion.*
>
> *The logistics of abundance call for mass production. This means the ascendancy of the machine. The risk of*

man's becoming subservient to it are great. The struggle of our time is to maintain an economy of plenty and yet keep man's freedom intact. Roadless areas are one pledge to freedom. With them intact, man need not become an automaton. There he can escape the machine and become once more a vital individual. If these inner sanctuaries are invaded by the machine, there is no escape. For men and civilization will be molded by mass compulsions.

Justice Douglas died in January 1980, at the age of eighty-one.

HARNESSING THE MIGHTY COLUMBIA

- 1942 -

AFTER ALMOST A DECADE OF DEDICATION AND HARD WORK, a group of engineers stood before a complex maze of switches, buttons, and controls in the powerhouse at Grand Coulee Dam. It was early June 1942. A jubilant crowd of ten thousand people gathered around the dam and its auxiliary structures to watch the gates on the dam open for the first time. The onlookers were proud to be at this dedication. Grand Coulee would soon be producing badly needed hydroelectric power for the war effort that had already sent hundreds of thousands of American men and women overseas.

When the long-awaited moment arrived, the controls were activated. Millions upon millions of gallons of water from the clear, cold Columbia River flooded over the spillway of the dam and plummeted to the river below in a steady stream measuring twice as high as Niagara Falls. Grand Coulee Dam, the largest concrete structure in the world, was officially on line.

Measuring 550 feet high and 4,173 feet long and containing more than 10 million cubic yards of concrete, Grand Coulee was almost four times longer than Hoover Dam in Arizona. It contained more than three times as much concrete as Hoover, which at the time of its completion in 1936 was the largest dam in the world. When reporters had queried him about Grand Coulee's immensity at the construction site five years earlier, an awed President Franklin D. Roosevelt had replied, "My head is full of figures and the easiest way to describe the figures is that this is the largest structure so far as anyone knows that has ever been undertaken by man." Grand Coulee's reservoir is just as monumental as the dam. Appropriately named Franklin Roosevelt Lake, it stretches 151 miles behind the dam, nearly to the Canadian border.

Although the mighty Grand Coulee project did not begin until 1933, the idea for such an undertaking had been around for at least fifteen years. Rufus Woods, the publisher of the small-town newspaper the *Wenatchee Daily World,* had advocated for such a structure in the region since 1918. When U.S. Senator Clarence Dill from Washington was reelected to office in 1928, most Washingtonians supported his pro-dam position. Some years later, Senator Dill recalled how he had approached the future president about the issue: "I first spoke to Franklin Roosevelt about Grand Coulee after dinner at his Hyde Park house in 1930—a year before he'd even declared he was running for President. He was blowing cigarette smoke and bubbling with ideas on how to halt the Great Depression."

Not long after Roosevelt took office in March 1933, he heeded Senator Dill's advice and allocated about $63 million for the construction of a low dam spanning the Columbia River. Members of Congress pouted for a while, dismayed that the new president hadn't even consulted them about the matter. After careful deliberation, however, Congress realized that such a hydroelectric project was needed for the Northwest and voted a generous $450 million to fund the construction of a high dam at the Grand Coulee of the Columbia.

Here, millions of years ago, an earlier version of the Columbia River had cut a fifty-mile-long canyon approximately one thousand feet deep in the basalt that formed the Northwest's Columbia Plateau. The place was ideal for a high-performance hydroelectric dam.

But Grand Coulee Dam was not the first engineering effort to harness the wild Columbia River. Bonneville Dam, located about halfway between Portland and The Dalles, was nearing completion in 1937. President Roosevelt took the occasion of the dedication of the Bonneville Dam to tour the Pacific Northwest. A *Time* magazine reporter who followed the presidential party wrote in the October 11, 1937, issue,

> *The president spent a week roving through the vast forests and high mountains of the most heroic terrain in the U.S. as though he had on [Paul] Bunyan's boots. Bonneville Dam, 170 ft. high, 1,250 ft. long is being built by War Department engineers complete with staircases as well as electric elevators for traveling salmon.*

At the dedication of the Bonneville Dam and powerhouse, Roosevelt took the opportunity to exalt his public projects program: "Instead of spending, as some nations do, half their national income in piling up armaments . . . we in America are wiser in using our wealth on projects like this which will give us more wealth, better living and great happiness for our children."

Draining an area as large as France, the Columbia River drops 2,650 feet along its 1,214-mile trip from Canada to the Pacific Ocean. Today, Grand Coulee and Bonneville are only two of several dams that tame this mighty stream and provide inexpensive electric power for the region's inhabitants.

THE SEATTLE WORLD'S FAIR

- 1962 -

It was Saturday, April 21, 1962, and thousands of spectators milled around the 607-foot-high Space Needle that had only recently been completed on the seventy-two-acre grounds of the Century 21 Exposition in Seattle. At the given time, President John F. Kennedy kicked off the fair's festivities by remotely activating the tower's carillon from Palm Beach, Florida. The bells began to chime, and the first world's fair to be held in the United States in twenty-two years was officially opened to one and all.

Previous world fairs in the United States, before the Seattle fair in 1962, were hosted by New York and San Francisco, in 1939 and 1940. Although war in Europe had been a constant threat at the time, the New York fair's futuristic theme of "The World of Tomorrow" had attracted nearly forty-five million visitors.

The concept of world fairs originated in medieval days when cities across Europe hosted trade fairs and invited merchants, craftsmen, and members of various guilds to display their wares. The fairs were joyous events, and people from miles around came, saw, and went home awed by the diversity of their fellows' output. The first truly international, or "world's," fair was held in London in 1851. After six million people had visited the eight miles of display tables, London's fair closed with a huge profit and a noticeable increase in requests for British goods.

Following London's success, other countries saw the benefit of hosting world fairs. Before the nineteenth century was over, several other expositions were held across the world, among them, New York City in 1853; Paris in 1855; South Kensington, England, in 1862; Paris again in 1867, 1878, and 1889; Philadelphia in 1866; and Chicago in 1893.

Promoters of the Seattle World's Fair looked to the future for their fair's theme. "Man in the Space Age" was a subject foremost in the minds of millions of Americans in the early 1960s, and the theme proved to be highly successful. Before the Seattle fair closed in October, nearly ten million people had visited its exhibits, each of them spending an average of five to six dollars. By September the four-million-dollar Space Needle had been paid for, primarily by the collected admission charges of one dollar for the elevator ride to the top.

The brain behind the Seattle World's Fair was Joseph E. Gandy, a former automobile dealer. Gandy emphasized the permanency of investment in the fair, even after it was long gone. "Eighty-five percent of every construction dollar has been permanently invested here," he preached. "We felt it was economically immoral to spend the taxpayers' money and not have something of lasting value come out of it." And indeed, the Space Needle and other exhibit areas are today part of the heritage of downtown Seattle.

The fair was built on a twenty-five-square-city-block area of Seattle bounded by Denny Way and Mercer Street on the south and north, and by First and Fifth Avenues North on the west and east.

Small when compared to other world fairs, the Seattle festivities nevertheless managed to feature a science pavilion the size of six football fields, an international mall, a 3,100-seat opera house, a 5,500-seat arena, a 20,000-seat coliseum, a food circus, a monorail terminal, an information center, a fine arts exhibit, an outdoor stadium, and more.

Journalists for *Time* magazine had nothing but praise for Seattle's efforts. After writing of Seattle officials' difficulties in getting the fair to their city (they "had to explain to many members of the Bureau of International Expositions that Seattle is not a part of Washington, D.C."), the *Time* correspondents continued:

> *Yet the Seattle fair, if not grandiose, is at least grand; it has a dignified, quiet beauty, a tidiness that will make it less tiresome than most world's fairs—and a core of common sense that reflects the Northwest's reluctance to waste its assets. When it closes on Oct. 21, most of its best features will remain to form a permanent $50 million civic center.*

In a later issue of *Time* published two months before the fair ended, the real importance of the exposition was revealed.

> *As for the rest of the fair, private creditors have already recouped their original $4,500,000 investment, and since the fair still has another two months to run, its promoters expect to wind up comfortably in the black. . . . The fair has given a lift to business throughout the Northwest, whose lumber and fishing industries have been hurting. Seattle restaurants are crowded, hotels*

> *have enjoyed 90% occupancy all summer—and motels en route, as far away as Butte, Mont., are usually full. . . . Seattle bankers estimate that the fair will add $160 million to Washington's economy this year.*

When the Seattle World's Fair closed to the public in October 1962, the experience provided one of the few instances on record in which such a grand undertaking not only paid for itself but also made a profit for its organizers.

THE ERUPTION OF MOUNT ST. HELENS

- 1980 -

It was Sunday morning, May 18, 1980. David Crockett, a photographer for station KOMO-TV in Seattle, stood at the base of 9,766-foot Mount St. Helens, a volcano in the Cascade Range that had been spewing fumes and lava since March 27. As he looked through the viewfinder of his camera, scanning the countryside for suitable footage for his producers, Crockett heard a deafening roar. In an instant a sea of mud was rushing toward him. He managed to get to a piece of dry land between two fingers of the mud river. As he watched in desperation, darkness closing in about him, he spoke into the camera's microphone:

> *I am walking toward the only light I can see. I can hear the mountain rumble. At this very moment I have to say, "Honest to God, I believe I am dead." The ash*

in my eyes burns my eyes, burns my eyes! Oh dear God this is hell! It's very, very hard to breathe and very dark. If I could only breathe air. God just give me a breath! I will try the radio. Mayday! Mayday! Ash is coming down on me heavily. It's either dark or I am dead. God, I want to live!

And, miraculously, Crockett did live, rescued by helicopter hours later. But at the same time Crockett was filming at Mount St. Helens's base, volcanologist David Johnston was five miles away observing the enlarged bulge that had appeared on the peak's slope. It was 8:31 a.m. when the eruption occurred, and Johnston managed to get a single message off on his radio before he was covered with ash and lava. "Vancouver! Vancouver! This is it!" were the last words the scientist uttered.

Moments later, in Spokane, Jean Penna was driving down the road from her apartment to her mother's house when the sky became foreboding. Penna later said, "In the time it took me to get from my apartment to my mother's house, it went black. All of a sudden this powder began to fall, just like snow. It was 75 degrees outside and pitch black."

And in far-off Missoula, Montana, a bewildered resident amid falling volcanic ash reported that he felt "like someone popped my eyeballs out and rolled them around in a sandbox."

The damage the May 1980 eruption of Mount St. Helens caused has been compared to the destruction inflicted by Italy's Mount Vesuvius, which unleashed its fury in A.D. 79. Mount St. Helens, now peaking at an elevation of 8,356 feet (it was 9,677 feet before the eruption), ejected at least 1½ cubic miles of lava and ash, destroying 150 square miles of timber in the process. In addition, alfalfa, wheat, and other crops were destroyed for miles around the mountain, and nearly six thousand miles of roads in the region were covered with ash. A twenty-mile-long logjam on the Columbia River paralyzed river traffic between Longview, Washington, and Astoria, Oregon. Portland's harbor was choked with mud, and volcanic ash darkened the skies over Washington and neighboring states for days. Salmon and trout died by the millions.

Mount St. Helens had been known to Americans since the earliest days of exploration in the Pacific Northwest. Captain Robert Gray observed the peak when he took his ship *Columbia* into the mouth of its namesake river. Lewis and Clark saw it on their expedition from St. Louis to the Pacific Ocean and back again in 1804–1806. The mountain received its name from British navigator Captain George Vancouver in October 1792. Alleyne Fitzherbert, or Baron St. Helens, the British ambassador to Spain at the time of Vancouver's travels, was the honoree.

Although less than forty thousand years old—fairly young for a volcano—Mount St. Helens had already had its share of turmoil. Indians in the region reported to British and American fur traders that the mountain had erupted many times in the past. And in 1857 it erupted again, although reported damage was minimal since the area was still a virtually uninterrupted wilderness.

As early as 1978 warnings had been issued that Mount St. Helens was a likely candidate for eruption in the not-too-distant future. On March 20, 1980, a series of earth tremors began northwest of the peak, followed by an actual eruption on March 27. Certain that bigger events were in store, scientists converged on Mount St. Helens by the droves, and Washington's governor, Dixy Lee Ray, issued evacuation orders for a large section of territory adjoining the mountain.

A few minutes after the 8:31 a.m. eruption, the skies filled with ash and dust. Debris flying at speeds estimated at 250 miles per hour shot from the volcano and traveled as far as seventeen miles. Dust and ash particles spewed twelve miles into the air as the aroused volcano vented its anger. Magnificent Douglas-fir and hemlock trees were uprooted and tossed about like matchsticks.

Unlike many of the world's disastrous volcano eruptions, the eruption of Mount St. Helens resulted in relatively few fatalities. Given Mount Vesuvius's death toll of two thousand, the 1902 Mount Pelée disaster that killed nearly thirty thousand inhabitants on the island of Martinique, or the 1883 Krakatoa eruption that claimed thirty-six thousand lives, the death toll at Mount St. Helens could have been far worse.

Today Mount St. Helens is quiet again, as sightseers walk along wooded trails and marvel at the reserved majesty of the mountain. The area around the volcano has been declared the Mount St. Helens National Volcanic Monument, thus echoing the words of President Jimmy Carter as he surveyed the aftermath in May 1980: "People will come from all over the world to observe the impressiveness of the force of nature. I would say it would be, if you'll excuse the expression, a tourist attraction that would equal the Grand Canyon."

THE SAGA OF KENNEWICK MAN

- 1996 -

SUNDAY, JULY 28, 1996, TURNED OUT TO BE A HOT, muggy day in the Tri-City area of Washington. Situated along the Columbia River just before the mighty stream makes a dramatic turn and heads rapidly for the Pacific Ocean nearly three hundred miles away to the west, Tri-Cities derives its name from the fact that three neighboring towns—Richland, Kennewick, and Pasco—nestle along the river for several miles just before the Snake River enters the Columbia from the east.

One of the premier summer events to take place in this part of south-central Washington is the Columbia Cup, a two-day world-class hydroplane race that attracts thousands of spectators from all over the Northwest. Many viewers observe the race from Columbia Park, a facility situated in Kennewick on the south bank of the Columbia and owned and operated by the Army Corps of Engineers. Around noon on that July 28, two college students were wandering about the remoter parts of Columbia Park, trying to find an easy entry (and a free one) into the spectators' section to watch the races. As they clambered along the river's banks, beneath some dense Russian olive trees, one of them spied a human skull staring at him from the muddy beach. Torn between whether to immediately report their find to local police or to hide the skull and continue watching the races until they were over later in the day, the youths decided on the latter option and proceeded to hide the skull in the thick undergrowth beneath the olive trees.

When the police were finally notified by the two students later in the afternoon, they called in Floyd Johnson, a retired homicide detective who was now serving as the Benton County coroner. Johnson made the short trip to Columbia Park, arriving at around six o'clock in the evening His initial assessment of the skull was that it was at least one hundred years old and that it most likely came from an Indian whose remains had been washed up by the river. But Johnson also realized that the remains needed to be studied by a professional, so he telephoned his friend and occasional colleague Dr. James G.

Chatters, an archaeologist and paleontologist who lived in nearby Richland. Chatters insisted that Johnson bring the remains to his house and basement laboratory, where, following a hurried examination, the scientist made a couple of astounding announcements: first, that the skull appeared to be at least five thousand years old (later radiocarbon analysis revealed it to be closer to 8,500 years old), and second, that the skull's features appeared to be more Caucasian than American Indian. Over the next few weeks, additional parts of the ancient man's body were recovered near where the skull had been found, and, when assembled, the pieces made a fairly complete specimen.

Within days after the news media learned of the skull's age, based on the radiocarbon analysis, a consortium of local Indian tribes—Wanapum, Colville, Nez Perce, Umatilla, and Yakima—declared that they intended to invoke the Native American Graves Protection and

Repatriation Act (NAGPRA) to take possession of all remains of "Kennewick Man," as the exciting find was now being called. NAGPRA became law in 1990, with the mandate to protect native burials on tribal and federally owned land and to provide a mechanism for the reclamation by the tribes of human remains and cultural artifacts that had previously been excavated and which currently resided in museums across the country. One of the tenets of the controversial legislation was that claimants to Indian remains and artifacts base their claim on the fact that the items in question were somehow "affiliated" with their tribe. Despite an outcry from scores of professional archaeologists that, because of the remains' antiquity, they could not possibly be affiliated with any historical Indian tribe, the Army Corps of Engineers, upon whose property the remains were found, initiated plans to turn them over to the tribal consortium.

As the Corps of Engineers prepared to transfer the Kennewick remains, eight eminent scientists filed suit to prohibit such action and asked to be allowed to conduct a full-scale anthropological investigation. In 1997 a federal court deferred the suit and ordered the corps to review its procedures for its earlier decision to turn over the remains. In March 1998 the corps and two partners in its mission, the U.S. Department of the Interior and one of its divisions, the National Park Service, hired their own panel of distinguished scientists to study the Kennewick site and its remains. During the following month, with the study complete, and without a similar study being allowed for the opposing side, the corps paid $160,000 to forever destroy the site by covering it with six hundred tons of rock, tree trunks, gravel, and dirt.

All the remains of Kennewick Man, in the meantime, were moved to the Burke Museum of Natural and Cultural History in Seattle, and the plaintiffs to the lawsuit were prohibited from studying them.

In September 2000 Secretary of the Interior Bruce Babbitt determined that Kennewick Man was culturally affiliated with the tribal consortium and that the skeletal remains should be awarded to the group for proper burial, effectively precluding any present or future scientific study. The earlier lawsuit was revived, and two years later Oregon's Ninth District Circuit Court overturned Babbitt's unilateral decision and authorized the plaintiffs to begin a study of the bones. Despite an appeal by the five interested Indian tribes, the Ninth Circuit Court of Appeals upheld the district court's ruling, declaring that the U.S. Government had failed to clearly demonstrate that Kennewick Man was an American Indian, thereby voiding the use of NAGPRA in the argument. Two months later the same court reaffirmed its earlier decision, thereby releasing the Kennewick remains to the plaintiffs for scientific study.

In February 2006, following several months of intensive study, anthropologists from the Smithsonian Institution, the University of Tennessee, and other noted scientific establishments discussed their preliminary findings at the annual meeting of the American Academy of Forensic Sciences, held that year in Seattle. The ancient age of the remains was confirmed, but the most intriguing of the questions—that of Kennewick Man's racial stock—is still being investigated. Preliminarily it appears that Kennewick's skull varies significantly from the skulls of the other, albeit few, Amerindians of the same age that have been excavated, thus setting the stage for all kinds of theories over just where this individual came from and how he ended up on this continent.

WASHINGTON FACTS AND TRIVIA

Washington is the twentieth-largest state in the nation. It encompasses 68,138 square miles, or almost 44 million acres. It measures 360 miles from east to west, and 240 miles from north to south.

The mean elevation of Washington is 1,700 feet. The highest point in the state is Mount Rainier, in Pierce County, with an altitude of 14,411 feet. The lowest point in the state is sea level on the Pacific coast.

The geographical center of Washington is ten miles west-southwest of Wenatchee in Chelan County.

The latest agricultural statistics show that Washington contains approximately 36,000 farms totaling about 15,318,000 acres, an average of 426 acres per farm.

The 2000 census revealed that Washington had a population of 5,894,121. The 2005 estimated population was 6,287,759.

The state ranks fifteenth in the nation for population.

The coldest temperature ever recorded in Washington was -48° Fahrenheit on December 30, 1968, at Mazama and Winthrop.

The hottest temperature was 118 degrees on August 5, 1961, at Ice Harbor Dam.

Washington became a U.S. territory in 1853. It became the forty-second state on November 1, 1889.

Olympia, with a 2003 estimated population of 43,963, is the capital of Washington. Seattle, with a 2003 estimated population of 569,101, is the state's largest city.

Washington contains thirty-nine counties.

Washington was named in honor of George Washington, first president of the United States.

The state motto is *Alki,* meaning "By and by."

Washington's official state nickname is the Evergreen State. It is also sometimes called the Chinook State.

The state bird is the willow goldfinch, also known as the American goldfinch *(Carduelis tristis).*

The state flower is the Pacific rhododendron *(Rhododendron macrophyllum),* and the state tree is the western hemlock *(Tsuga heterophylla).*

The state gemstone is petrified wood.

The state fish is the steelhead trout *(Onchorhynchus mykiss).*

The state song is "Washington My Home," by Helena Davis.

The state flag consists of the state seal on a green field. It is the only state flag to display a portrait (George Washington) and the only one with a green field.

BIBLIOGRAPHY

Bakeless, John. *The Eyes of Discovery.* Philadelphia: J. B. Lippincott, 1950.

Barry, Louise. *The Beginning of the West.* Topeka: Kansas Historical Society, 1972.

Biddle, Nicholas, ed. *The Journals of the Expedition under the Command of Capts. Lewis and Clark, 1814.* Reprint, New York: Heritage Press, 1962.

Bledsoe, Helen Wieman. "The Generous People of Cape Flattery." *Old West* 30 (3):40–45, 1994.

Castor, Henry. *"Fifty-Four Forty or Fight!"* New York: Franklin Watts, 1970.

Chatters, J. C. *Ancient Encounters: Kennewick Man and the First Americans.* New York: Simon & Schuster, 2001.

Dodd, Jack. "The Indians Have an Inning." *Great Western Indian Fights.* Compiled by Potomac Corral of the Westerners. Lincoln: University of Nebraska Press, n.d.

Douglas, William O. *Go East, Young Man.* New York: Random House, 1974.

———. *My Wilderness.* Garden City, N.J.: Doubleday, 1960.

Drury, Clifford M. *Marcus and Narcissa Whitman and the Opening of Old Oregon.* Glendale, Calif.: Arthur H. Clark Co., 1973.

Dryden, Cecil. *Up the Columbia for Furs.* Caldwell, Idaho: Caxton Printers, 1949.

"Fair Weather in Seattle." *Time* (August 1962): 76.

Flight Path: A History of the Boeing Company. Seattle: Boeing Company, 1991.

Friedheim, Robert L. *The Seattle General Strike.* Seattle: University of Washington Press, 1964.

"God, I Want to Live!" *Time* (June 1980): 26–35.

Goetzmann, William H. *Army Exploration in the American West 1803–1863.* Lincoln: University of Nebraska Press, 1979.

"Go West Everybody." *Time* (April 1962): 60–65.

Holbrook, Stewart H. *Burning an Empire: The Story of American Forest Fires.* New York: Macmillan, 1945.

———. *The Columbia River.* New York: Holt, Rinehart & Winston, 1965.

Horan, James D., and Paul Sann. *Pictorial History of the Wild West.* New York: Crown Publishers, 1954.

Jackson, Donald, and Mary Lee Spence, eds. *The Expeditions of John Charles Frémont.* Vol. 1. Urbana: University of Illinois Press, 1970.

"The Judiciary." *Time* (March 1939): 12–13.

Judson, Katharine B. *Early Days in Old Oregon.* Chicago: A. C. McClurg & Co., 1916.

Lavender, David. "Point of Genesis." In *Fort Vancouver.* Handbook 113. Washington, D.C.: Division of Publications, National Park Service, 1981.

———. *The Way to the Western Sea.* New York: Harper & Row, 1988.

Martinson, Arthur. *Wilderness above the Sound.* Flagstaff, Ariz.: Northland Press, n.d.

McKay, Charles. "History of San Juan Island." *Washington Historical Quarterly.* 2 (4).

Meyers, Rex C. "The Mullan Road." *Pioneer Trails West,* edited by Don Worcester. Caldwell, Idaho: Caxton Printers,1985.

"Military Road from Fort Benton to Fort Walla-Walla." House Executive Document No. 44. Thirty-sixth Congress, second session. Washington, D.C., 1861.

Montgomery, Elizabeth Rider. *When a Ton of Gold Reached Seattle.* Champaign, Ill.: Garrard Publishing, 1968.

Morgan, Murray. *The Columbia: Powerhouse of the West.* Seattle: Superior Publishing, 1949.

Moulton, Gary E., ed. *The Journals of the Lewis & Clark Expedition.* Vols. 5 (1988) and 6 (1990). Lincoln: University of Nebraska Press, 1983–2001.

"Our National Parks." *Reader's Digest.* Pleasantville, N.Y.: The Reader's Digest Association, 1985.

Peltier, Jerome. "Ross Cox." In *The Mountain Men and the Fur Trade of the Far West,* edited by LeRoy R. Hafen. Vol. 7. Glendale, Calif.: Arthur H. Clark Co., 1969.

"The Presidency." *Time* (October 1937): 14.

"The Presidency." *Time* (February 1939): 13–14.

Reavis, L. U. *The Life and Military Services of Gen. William Selby Harney.* St. Louis: Bryan, Brand & Co., 1878.

Sheffield, Delia B. "Reminiscences of Delia B. Sheffield." *Washington Historical Quarterly* 15 (1).

Stewart, Edgar I. "Alexander Ross." In *The Mountain Men and the Fur Trade of the Far West,* edited by LeRoy R. Hafen. Vol. 6. Glendale, Calif.: Arthur H. Clark Co., 1969.

Utley, Robert M., and Wilcomb E. Washburn. *The American Heritage History of the Indian Wars.* New York: American Heritage Publishing Co., 1977.

Viola, Herman J., and Carolyn Margolis, eds. *Magnificent Voyagers: The U.S. Exploring Expedition, 1838–1842.* Washington, D.C.: Smithsonian Institution Press, 1985.

Williams, Richard L. *The Loggers.* Alexandria, Va.: Time-Life Books, 1976.

———. *The Northwest Coast.* New York: Time-Life Books, 1973.

INDEX

ABOUT THE AUTHOR

James A. Crutchfield is the author of forty books dealing with various aspects of American history. He is the author of eight titles in the popular "It Happened In . . . " series: Montana, Colorado, Washington, Oregon, Arizona, New Mexico, Texas, and Georgia. He has contributed hundreds of articles to newspapers, journals, and national magazines such as *The Magazine Antiques, Early American Life,* and *The American Cowboy.*

Crutchfield's writing achievements have been recognized with awards from the Western Writers of America, the American Association for State and Local History, and the Tennessee Revolutionary Bicentennial Commission. A former board member of the Tennessee Historical Society, he presently sits on the Board of National Scholars for President's Park in Williamsburg, Virginia. He and his wife, Regena, reside in a pre–Civil War home in Tennessee.